Table of Contents

Title

Crime Cases on Monday

By Ryder Clerk

Chapter No 1: The Man with the Cough

I'm a German by birth and descent. My name is Schmidt. But by education I'm relatively as much an Englishman as a' Deutscher', and by affection much more the former. My life has been spent enough inversely between the two countries, and I flatter myself I speak both languages without any foreign accentuation.

I count England my headquarters now it's' home' to me. But a many times ago I was resident in Germany, only going over to London now and also on business. I'll not mention the city where I lived. It's gratuitous to do so, and in the peculiar experience I'm about to relate I suppose real names of people and places are just as well, or better avoided.

I was connected with a large and important establishment of masterminds. I had been bred up to the profession, and was credited with a certain quantum of' gift; and I was considered- and, with all modesty, I suppose I merited the opinion-steady and dependable, so that I had formerly attained a fair position in the house, and was looked upon as a" rising man'. But I was still youthful, and not relatively so wise as I allowed myself. I came veritably near formerly to making a great mess of a certain affair. It's this story which I'm going to tell.

Our house went in largely for patents- rather too largely, some study. But the head mate's son was a bit of a genius in his way, and his father was growing old, and let Herr Wilhelm-Moritz we will call the family name- do enough much as he chose. Overall Herr Wilhelm did well. He was conservative, and he had the benefit of the still lesser caution and larger experience of Herr Gerhardt, the alternate mate in the establishment.

Patents and the laws which regulate them are queer effects to have to do with. No bone who has not had particular experience of the complications that arise could believe how far these spread and how entangled they come. Great acuteness as well as caution is called for if you would guide your patent dinghy safely to harborage- and maybe further than anything, a power of holding your lingo. I was no talker, nor, when on a charge of significance, did I go about looking as if I were bursting with secrets, which is, in my opinion, nearly as dangerous as revealing them. No bone, to meet me on the peregrinations which it frequently fell to my lot to take over, would have guessed that I had anything on my mind but an easy- going youthful fellow's natural interest in his surroundings, however numerous a time I've stayed awake through a whole night of road trip if at all doubtful about my fellow- passengers, or not dared to go to sleep in a hostel without a ready-loaded revolver by my pillow. For now and also- however not through me- our secrets did slush out. And if, as has happed, they were secrets connected with Government orders or contracts, there was, or but for the exertion of the topmost energy and tactfulness on the part of my elders, there would have been, to put it plainly, the devil to pay.

One morning- it was nearing the end of November I was transferred for to Herr Wilhelm's private room. There I set up him and Herr Gerhardt before a table spread with papers covered with numbers and computations, and wastes of beautifully executed plates.

Lutz,' said Herr Wilhelm. He'd known me from nonage, and frequently called me by the condensation of my Christian name, which is Ludwig, or Louis.' Lutz, we're going to entrust to you a matter of extreme significance. You must be prepared to start for London hereafter.'

All right, joe,' I said,' I shall be ready.'

You'll take the express through to Calais- on the whole it's the stylish route, especially at this season. By travelling all night you'll catch the boat there, and arrive in London so as to have a good night's rest, and be clear- headed for work the coming morning.'

I bowed agreement, but ventured to make a suggestion. Still, as I infer, the matter is one of great significance,' If.' Herr Wilhelm looked at Herr Gerhardt. Herr Gerhardt shook his head.

No,' he replied,' hereafter it must be,' and also he progressed to explain to me why.

I need not essay to give all the details of the matter with which I was entrusted. Indeed, to' lay' compendiums it would be insolvable. Serve it to say, the whole concerned a patent- that of a veritably remarkable and awful invention, which it was hoped and believed the Government of both countries would take up. But to secure this being done in a completely satisfactory manner it was necessary that our establishment should go about it in musicale with an English house of first- rate standing. To this house the establishment of Messrs Bluestone & Fagg I'll call them- I was to be transferred with full explanations. And the coming half- hour or further passed in my elders going roundly into the details, so as to satisfy themselves that I understood. The mastering of the total wasn't delicate, for I was well predicated technically; and like numerous of the stylish effects the idea was basically simple, and the plates were perfect. When the explanations were over, and my instructions properly noted, I began to gather together the colorful wastes, which were each numbered. But, to my surprise, Herr Gerhardt, looking over me, withdrew two of the most important plates, without which the others were chaffy, because unexplainable.

'Stay,' he said;' these two, Ludwig, must be kept separate. These we shoot moment, by registered post, direct to Bluestone & Fagg. They will admit them a day before they see you, and with them a letter publicizing your appearance.'

I looked up in some disappointment. I had known of preventives of the kind being taken, but generally when the hand transferred was less dependable than I believed myself to be. Still, I scarcely dared to objection.

'Do you suppose that necessary?' I said hypercritically.' I can assure you that from the moment you entrust me with the papers they shall noway quit me day or night. And if there were any postal detention you say time is precious in this case- or if the papers were stolen in the conveyance- similar effects have happed- my whole charge would be empty.

We don't misdoubt your zeal and discretion, my good Schmidt,' said Herr Gerhardt.' But in this case we must take indeed redundant preventives. I hadn't meant to tell you, stewing to add to the certain quantum of unease and strain necessary in such a case, but still, maybe it's stylish that you should know that we've reason for some special anxiety. It has been suggested to us that some breath of this'- and he tapped the papers-' has reached those who are always on the watch for similar effects. We can not be too careful.'

'And yet', I persisted,' you would trust the post?'

We don't trust the post,' he replied.' Indeed if these plates were tampered with, they would be impeccably useless. And tampered with they won't be. But indeed supposing anything so wild, the hellions in question knowing of your departure(and they're more likely to know of it than of our packet by post), were they in conspiracy with some snake in the post office, are sharp enough to guess the verity- that we've made a Masonic secret of it- the two separate plates are chaffy without your papers; your papers reveal nothing without Nos. 7 and 13.'

I bowed in submission. But I was, all the same, disappointed, as I said, and a trifle rattled.

Herr Wilhelm saw it, and cheered me up.

'All right, Lutz, my boy,' he said.' I feel just like you- nothing I should enjoy further than a rush over to London, carrying the whole documents, and prepared for a fight with anyone who tried to get hold of them. But Herr Gerhardt then's cooler- thoroughbred than we are.'

The elder man smiled.

'I do not misdoubt your readiness to fight, nor Ludwig's moreover. But it would be by no similar actually brutal means as open thievery that we should be outsmarted. Make musketeers readily with no bone while travelling, Lutz, yet avoid the appearance of keeping yourself frosty. You understand?'

Impeccably,' I said.' I shall sleep well tonight, so as to be prepared to keep awake throughout the trip.'

The papers were also precisely packed up. Those consigned to my care were to be carried in a certain light, black handbag with a veritably good cinch, which had frequently ahead been my travelling companion. And the ensuing evening I started by the express train agreed upon. So, at least, I've always believed, but I've noway been suitable to bring forward a substantiation to the fact of my train at the launch being the right one, as no bone came with me to see me off. For it was allowed stylish that I should depart in as invisible a manner as possible, as, indeed in a large city similar as ours, the members and workers of an old and important house like the Moritzes' were well known.

I took my ticket also, registering no luggage, as I had none but what I fluently carried in my hand, as well as the bag. It was formerly dusk, if not dark, and there wasn't important bustle in the station, nor supposedly numerous passengers. I took my place in an empty alternate- class cube, and sat there still till the train should start. A many twinkles before it did another man got in. I was kindly irked at this, as in my circumstances nothing was more undesirable than travelling alone with one other. Had there been a crowded cube, or one with three or four passengers, I would have chosen it; but at the moment I got in, the carriages were each moreover empty or with but one or two inhabitants. Now, I said to myself, I should have done better to stay till nearer the time of departure, and also chosen my place.

I turned to fathom my companion, but I couldn't see his face easily, as he was partial leaning out of the window. Was he doing so on purpose? I said to myself, for naturally I was in a suspicious mood. And as the study struck me I half started up, determined to choose another cube. Suddenly a peculiar sound made itself heard. My companion was coughing. He drew his head in, covering his face with his hand, as he coughed again. You noway heard such a curious cough. It was more like a hen clucking than anything I can suppose of. Formerly, doubly he coughed; also, as if he'd been staying for the slight spasm to pass, he sprang up, looked eagerly out of the window again, and, opening the door, jumped out, with some interjection, as if he'd just caught sight of a friend.

And in another moment or two- he could slightly have had time to get in away- important to my satisfaction, the train moved off.

Now,' allowed I,' I can make myself comfortable for some hours. We don't stop till M---- it'll be nine o'clock by then. However, and a clear run to Calais, If no bone gets in there I'm safe to go through till hereafter alone; also there will only be---- Junction.'

I unstrapped my hairpiece and lit a cigar- of course I had chosen a smoking- carriage- and, pleased at having got relieve of my clucking companion, the time passed pleasantly till we pulled up at M----. The detention there wasn't great, and to my enormous satisfaction no bone molested my solitariness. Putatively the express to Calais wasn't in veritably great demand that night. I now felt so secure that, notwithstanding my intention of keeping awake all night, my inmost knowledge hadn't I suppose relatively abnegated itself to the necessity, for, not further than a hour or so after leaving M----, conceivably sooner, I fell presto asleep.

It sounded to me that I had slept heavily, for when I awoke I had great difficulty in flashing back where I was. Only by slow degrees did I realize that I wasn't in my comfortable bed at home, but in a chilly, ill- lighted road- carriage. Chilly- yes, that it was- veritably chilly; but as my faculties returned I flashed back my precious bag, and forgot all additional in a evanescent terror that it had been taken from me. No; there it was my elbow had been pressed against it as I slept. But how was this? The train wasn't in stir. We were standing in a station; a dingy vacated looking place, with no cheerful noise or bustle; only one or two janitors sluggishly moving about, with a kind of sleepy' night duty', surly air. It couldn't be the Junction? I looked at my watch. Slightly night! Of course, not the Junction. We weren't due there till four-o'clock in the morning or so.

What, also, were we doing then, and what was' then'? Had there been an accident- some unlooked-for necessity for stopping? At that moment a curious sound, from some yards' distance only it sounded to come, caught my observance. It was that claiming, roaring cough!- the cough of my evanescent fellow- passenger, towards whom I had felt an spontaneous aversion. I looked out of the window- there was a refreshment room just opposite, dimly lighted, like everything differently, and in the doorway, as if just entering, was a figure which I felt enough sure was that of the man with the cough.

Bah!' I said to myself,' I mustn't be fantastic. I dare say the fellow's each right. He's putatively in the same hole as myself. What in Heaven's name are we staying then for?'

I sprang out of the carriage, nearly tumbling over a gatekeeper sluggishly passing on.

How long are we to stay then?' I cried.' When do we start again for----?' and I named the Junction.

'For----,' he repeated in the queerest German I ever heard was it German? Or did I discover his meaning by some preternatural cleverness of my own?' There's no train for---- for four or five hours, not till----' and he named the time; and leaning forward lazily, he took out my larger bag and my hairpiece, depositing them on the platform. He didn't feel the least surprised at chancing me there I might have been there for a week, it sounded to me.

No train for five hours? Are you frenetic?' I said.

He shook his head and grunted commodity, and it sounded to me that he refocused to the refreshment- room contrary. Gathering my effects together I hastened thither, hoping to find some further dependable authority. But there was no bone there except a fat man with a white apron, who was clearing the counter- and- yea, in one corner was the figure I had mentally dubbed' The man with the cough'.

I addressed the chef or server- whichever he was. But he only shook his head- denied all knowledge of the trains, but informed me that- in other words- I must turn out; he was going to shut up.

And where am I to spend the night, also?' I said angrily, though easily it wasn't the aproned existent who was responsible for the position in which I set up myself.

There was a' Restauration', he informed me, near at hand, which I should find still open, straight before me on leaving the station, and also a many doors to the right, I would see the lights.

Easily there was nothing differently to be done. I went out, and as I did so the silent figure in the corner rose also and followed me. The station was putatively going to bed. As I passed the gatekeeper I repeated the hour he'd named, adding' That's the first train for---- Junction?'

He jounced, again naming the exact time. But I can not do so, as I've noway been suitable to recollect it.

I trudged along the road- there were lights, though veritably delicate bones; but by their light I saw that the man who had been in the refreshment- room was still a many way behind me. It made me feel slightly nervous, and I looked round furtively formerly or doubly; the last time I did so he wasn't to be seen, and I hoped he'd gone some other way.

The' Restauration' was scarcely further inviting than the station- room. It, too, was veritably dimly lighted, and the one or two attendants sounded partial asleep and were strangely silent. There was a fire of a kind, and I seated myself at a small table near it and asked for some coffee, which would, I allowed, serve the double purpose of warming me and keeping me awake.

It was brought me, in silence. I drank it, and felt the better for it. But there was commodity so caliginous and offish, so queer and nearly weird about the whole aspect and feeling of the place, that a kind of perverse abdication took possession of me. However, neither will I, I said to myself childishly, If these surly folk will not speak. And, inconceivable as it may sound, I didn't speak. I suppose I paid for the coffee, but I'm not relatively sure. I know I noway asked what I had meant to ask- the name of the city- a place of some significance, to judge by the size of the station and the extent of twinkling lights I had observed as I made my way to the' Restauration'. From that day to this I've noway been suitable to identify it, and I'm relatively sure I noway shall.

What was there peculiar about that coffee? Or was it commodity peculiar about my own condition that caused it to have the unusual effect I now endured? That question, too, I can not answer. All I flash back is feeling a sensation of infectious doziness creeping over me- internal, or moral I may say, as well as physical. For when one part of me perceptibly defied the first rush of sleep, commodity sounded to reply' Oh, gibberish! You have several hours before you. Your papers are each right. No bone can touch them without awaking you.'

And dreamily conscious that my things were on the bottom at my bases the bag itself actually resting against my ankle- my scruples silenced themselves in an extraordinary way. I flash back nothing further, save a vague knowledge through all my slumber of confused and chaotic dreams, which I've noway been suitable to recall.

I awoke at last, and that with a launch, nearly a haul. Commodity had awakened me- a sound- and as it was repeated to my now aroused cognizance I knew that I had heard it ahead, out and on, during my sleep. It was the extraordinary cough!

I looked up. Yes, there he was! At some two or three yards' distance only, at the other side of the fireplace, which, and this I've forgotten to mention as another peculiar item in that night's peculiar gests , considering I've every reason to believe I was still in Germany, wasn't a cook stove, but an open grate.

And he hadn't been there when I first fell asleep; to that I was prepared to swear.

He must have come sneaking in after me,' I allowed, and in all probability I should neither have noticed nor recognized him but for that treacherous chuckle of his.

Now, my misgivings aroused, my first study, of course, was for my precious charge. I deigned. There were my hairpieces, my larger bag, but- no, not the lower one; and though the other two were there, I knew at formerly that they weren't relatively in the same position- not so close to me. Horror seized me. Half hectically I peered around, when my silent neighbor fraudulent towards me. I could declare there was nothing in his hand when he did so, and I could declare as appreciatively that I had formerly looked under the small round table beside which I sat, and that the bag wasn't there. And yet when the man, with a slight chuckle, caused, no mistrustfulness, by his stooping, raised himself, the thing was in his hand!

Was he a conjuror, a pupil of Maskelyne and Cook? And how was it that, indeed as he held out my missing property, he managed, and that utmost cleverly and unobtrusively, to help my catching sight of his face! I didn't see it also- I noway did see it!

Commodity he muttered, to the effect that he supposed the bag was what I was looking for. In what language he spoke I know not; it was more that by the action accompanying the grunted sounds, I gathered his meaning, than that I heard anything eloquent.

I thanked him, of course, mechanically, so to say, though I began to feel as if he were an evil spirit hanging me. I could only hope that the splendid cinch to the bag had defied all curiosity, but I felt in a fever to be alone again, and suitable to satisfy myself that nothing had been tampered with.

The study recalled my wandering faculties. How long had I been asleep? I drew out my watch. Welkin! It was close upon the hour named for the first train in the morning. I sprang up, collected my effects, and dashed out of the' Restauration'. Still, I clearly didn't pay for it also, If I hadn't paid for my coffee ahead. Besides my haste, there was another reason for this- there was no bone to pay to! Not a critter was to be seen in the room or at the door as I passed out- always excepting the man with the cough.

As I left the place and hastened along the road, a bell began, not to ring, but to risk. It sounded most uncanny. What it meant, of course, I've noway known. It may have been a process to the workpeople of some plant, it may have been like all the other gests of that strange night. But no; this proposition I'll not at present enter upon.

Dawn wasn't yet breaking, but there was in one direction a faint suggestion of commodity of the kind not far out. Else all was dark. I stumbled along as stylish as I could, helped in reality, I suppose, by the unattractive unheroic hint of the woebegone road, or road lights. And it wasn't far to the station, though ever it sounded further than when I came; and ever, too, it sounded to have grown steep, though I couldn't flash back having noticed any pitch the other way on my appearance. A agony- suchlike sensation began to oppress me. I felt as if my luggage was growing shortly heavier and heavier, as if I should noway reach the station; and to this was joined the agonizing terror of missing the train.

I made a hopeless trouble. Cold as it was, the globules of perspiration stood out upon my forepart as I forced myself on. And by degrees the agony feeling cleared off. I set up myself entering the station at a run just as- yea, a train was actually beginning to move! I dashed, baggage and all, into a cube; it was empty, and it was a alternate- class one, precisely analogous to the bone

I had enthralled ahead; it might have been the veritably same one. The train gradationally increased its speed, but for the first many moments, while still in the station and passing through its immediate cortege , another strange thing struck me- the extraordinary silence and death of all about. Not one mortal being did I see, no gatekeeper watching our departure with the faithful though stolid interest always to be seen on the gatekeeper's visage. I might have been alone in the train it might have had a freight of the dead, and been itself propelled by some supernatural agency, so distinctly, so gloomily did it do.

You'll scarcely credit that I actually and for the third time fell asleep. I couldn't help it. Some occult influence was at work upon me throughout those dark hours, I'm appreciatively certain. And with the daylight it was disbanded. For when I again awoke I felt for the first time since leaving home fully and typically myself, fresh and vigorous, all my faculties at their stylish.

But, nonetheless, my first sensation was a launch of amazement, nearly of terror. The cube was nearly full! There were at least five or six trippers besides myself, veritably respectable, ordinary- looking folk, with nothing in the least intimidating about them. Yet it was with a rustle of extraordinary relief that I set up my precious bag in the corner beside me, where I had precisely placed it. It was concealed from view. No bone, I felt assured, could have touched it without awaking me.

It was broad and bright daylight. How long had I slept?

'Can you tell me,' I enquired of my contrary neighbour, a cheery- faced compatriot-' Can you tell me how soon we get to Junction by this train? I'm most anxious to catch the evening correspondence at Calais, and am relatively out in my reckonings, owing to an extraordinary detention at---- I've wasted the night by getting into a stopping train rather of the express.'

He looked at me in astonishment. He must have allowed me either frenetic or just awaking from a fit of intoxication- only I flatter myself I didn't look as if the ultimate were the case.

How soon we get to---- Junction?' he repeated.' Why, my good joe, you left it about three hours agone! It's now eight o'clock. We all got in at the Junction. You were alone, if I mistake not?'- he glanced at one or two of the others, who championed his statement.' And veritably presto asleep you were, and must have been, not to be disturbed by the bustle at the station. And as for catching the evening boat at Calais'- he burst into a loud giggle-' why, it would be veritably hard lines to do no better than that! We all hope to cross by the noon one.'

Also- what train is this?' I blatted, hugely nonplussed.

The express, of course. All of us, excepting yourself, joined it at the Junction,' he replied.

The express?' I repeated.' The express that leaves'- and I named my own city- at six in the evening?'

Exactly. You have got into the right train after all,' and then came another cry of recreation.' How did you suppose we had all got in if you hadn't yet passed the Junction? You hadn't the pleasure of our company from M----, I take it? M----, which you passed at nine o'clock last night, if my memory is correct.'

Also', I persisted, this is the double fast express, which doesn't stop between M---- and your Junction?'

Exactly,' he repeated; and also, verified most presumably in his belief that I was frenetic, or the other thing, he turned to his review, and left me to my extraordinary cogitations.

Had I been featuring? Insolvable! Every sensation, the veritably taste of the coffee, sounded still present with me the curious accentuation of the officers at the mysterious city, I could impeccably recall. I still fiddled at the remembrance of the chilly waking in the' Restauration'; I heard again the roaring cough.

But I felt I must collect myself, and be ready for the important concession entrusted to me. And to do this I must for the time banish these fruitless sweats at working the problem.

We had a good run to Calais, set up the boat in staying, and a fair passage brought us prosperously across the Channel. I set up myself in London immediate to the willed hour of my appearance.

At formerly I drove to the diggingsin a small road off the beachfront which I was oriented to frequent in similar circumstances. I felt nervous till I had an occasion of completely catching my documents. The Custom House officers had opened the bag, but the words' private papers' had served to help any farther examination; and to my inenarrable delight they were complete. A regard satisfied me as to this the moment I got them out, for they were most precisely numbered.

The coming morning saw me beforehand on my way to-No. 909, we will say- Black friars Street, where was the office of Messrs Bluestone & Fagg. I had noway been there ahead, but it was easy to find, and had I felt any doubt, their name goggled me in the face at the side of the open doorway.' Alternate- bottom' I allowed I read; but when I reached the first wharf I imagined I must have been incorrect. For there, at a door ajar, stood an eminently respectable- looking gentleman, who bowed as he saw me, with a discreet smile.

Herr Schmidt?' he said.' Ah, yes; I was on the lookout for you.'

I felt a little surprised, and my regard inevitably erred to the doorway. There was no name upon it, and it appeared to have been lately painted. My new friend saw my regard.

It's each right,' he said;' we have the painters then. We are using these lower apartments temporarily. I was watching to help your having the trouble of mounting to the alternate- bottom.'

And as I followed him in, I caught sight of a painter's graduation- a small one- on the stair over, and the smell was also unmistakable. The large external office looked bare and empty, but under the circumstances that was natural. No bone was, at the first regard, to be seen; but behind a dulled glass partition webbing off one corner I fancied I caught sight of a seated figure. And an inner office, to which my captain led the way, had a more comfortable and inhabited look. Then stood a youngish man. He bowed politely.

Mr. Fagg, my inferior,' said the first individual perkily.' And now, Herr Schmidt, to business at formerly, if you please. Time is everything. You have all the documents ready?'

I answered by opening my bag and spreading out its contents. Both men were veritably grave, nearly dumb; but as I progressed to explain effects it was easy to see that they completely understood all I said.

And now,' I went on, when I had reached a certain point,' if you'll give me Nos. 7 and 13 which you have formerly entered by registered post, I can put you in full possession of the whole. Without them, of course, all I've said is, so to say, primary only.'

The two looked at each other.

Of course,' said the elder man,' I follow what you say. The key of the total is wanting. But I was shortly awaiting you to bring it out. We haven't- Fagg, I'm right, am I not- we've entered nothing by post?'

Nothing whatever,' replied his inferior. And the answer sounded simplicity itself. Why did a strange exhilaration of misgiving go through me? Was it commodity in the look that had passed between them? Maybe so. In any case, strange to say, the inconsistency between their having entered no papers and yet looking for my appearance at the hour mentioned in the letter accompanying the documents, and accosting me by name, didn't strike me till some hours latterly.

I threw off what I believed to be my ridiculous distrust, and it wasn't delicate to do so in my extreme annoyance.

I can not understand it,' I said.' It's really too bad. Everything depends upon 7 and 13. I must reply at formerly for enquiries to be introduced at the post office.'

But your people must have duplicates,' said Fagg eagerly.' These can be encouraged at formerly.'

I hope so,' I said, though feeling strangely confused and upset.

They must shoot them direct then,' he went on.

I didn't at formerly answer. I was gathering my papers together.

And in the meantime', he progressed, touching my bag, you had better leave these then. We'll lock them up in the safe at formerly. It's better than carrying them about London.'

It clearly sounded so. I half laid down the bag on the table, but at that moment from the external room a most peculiar sound caught my cognizance- a faint cackling cough! I suppose I concealed my launch. I turned away as if considering Fagg's suggestion, which, to confess the verity, I had been on the veritably point of agreeing to. For it would have been a great relief to me to know that the papers were in safe guardianship. But now a flash of lurid light sounded to have converted everything.

I thank you,' I replied,' I should be glad to be free from the responsibility of the charge, but I dare not let these out of my own hands till the agreement is formally inked.'

The youngish man's face darkened. He assumed a bullying tone.

I do not know how it strikes you, Mr. Bluestone,' he said,' But it seems to me that this youthful gentleman is going rather too far. Do you suppose your employers will be pleased to hear of your affronting us, joe?'

But the elder man smiled condescendingly, however with a touch of superciliousness. It was veritably well done. He gestured his hand.

Stay, my dear Mr. Fagg; we can well go to make allowance. You'll reply at formerly, no mistrustfulness, Herr Schmidt, and- let me see- yes, we shall admit the duplicates ofNos. 7 and 13 by first post on Thursday morning.'

I bowed. Exactly,' I replied, as I lifted the now locked bag.' And you may anticipate me at the same hour on Thursday morning.'

Also I took my departure, accompanied to the door by the smooth existent who had entered me.

The telegram which I at formerly dispatched wasn't couched precisely as he'd have mandated, I allow. And he'd have been vastly surprised at my transferring off another, latterly in the day, to Bluestone & Fagg's apothegmatic address, in these words Ineluctably detained till Thursday morning. – SCHMIDT.'

This was after the appearance of a line from home in answer to mine. By Thursday morning I had had time to admit a letter from Herr Wilhelm, and to secure the services of a certain noted operative, accompanied by whom I presented myself at the appointed hour at 909. But my companion's services weren't needed. The catcalls had flown, advised by the same snake in our camp through whom the first hints of the new patent had blurted out. With him it was easy to deal, poor wretch! But the clever hellions who had employed him and impersonated the members of the honorable establishment of Bluestone & Fagg were noway traced.

The concession was successfully carried out. The experience I had gone through left me a wiser man. It's to be hoped, too, that the possessors of 909 Black friars Street were more conservative in the future as to whom they let their demesne to when temporarily vacant. The repainting of the door way etc., at the tenant's own expenditure had formerly roused some slight dubitation.

It's dispensable to add that Nos. 7 and 13 had been properly entered on the alternate-bottom.

I've noway known the true history of that extraordinary night. Was it all a dream, or a predictive vision of warning? Or was it in any sense true? Had I, in some unexplainable way, left my own city before than I intended, and really travelled in a slow train?

Or had the man with a cough, for his own unrighteous purposes, mesmerized or hypnotized me, and to some extent succeeded? I can not say. Occasionally, indeed, I ask myself if I'm relatively sure that there ever was similar a person as' the man with the cough'!

Chapter No. 2: Why Am I Here?

I wonder if I was always then? Sitting on this bench, gaping frenetically in hunt for some hinterland Nazi law enforcement, searching for some bewildered fugitive. I flash back when I was youthful, I used to just sit at home, wonder if this was all then before me, if there was indeed a world before I was then. Perhaps there was nothing, perhaps there was so much more. The stories my grandpa used to tell made me feel I'd missed everything. A world drenched is some acid washed insanity, on a psychedelic surge of peace and love. The world was some schizophrenic sociopath, that set up it's cool long before I was then, now life sits in its monotonous way in respect to its audacious path, unfit to live up to its former tone. And yet flashes pass over me in a surge of sickness and dysphoria.

It's weird how you concentrate on little effects, indeed in big moments, insane moments, that ever break down to the smells in the room. The wind on a lip, as your cold arm of death wields an extension of it's will. You do not see the moment for the wholeness of its meaning, just the corridor that made it's horror sufferable. The ease I felt reliving this, came a shiver crawling up my chine, chilling the bone as my body jounced in nausea. Where am I? Bus stop, 343 am. City conveyance may be a miraculous product of megacity living, but it's not for the benefit of brutes of the night. I find myself floundering to fight lumping myself into that group, more and more as the times go by.

I wonder if that is how nonnatives look at us, do they see what is sitting below the face? Staying to peep behind our covers, staying to vault over the hedge and unleash it's will. It's sad that I find this further apt to myself than anything differently, there was commodity I wouldn't have conceded before the moments that I was reeling from. Riots, the room's shrouded in a fuzzy haze of treble mutters & expressions of terror, and misprision. I watch myself in this moment, a sterile green gleam filled the store, that cool buzz from the chilling units of the reverse wall created a nauseating hum in the reverse of your cranium. The wobbling drilling holes into your brain, you could feel, smell the anxiety in the air like the fresh scent of sick and dirt sitting on your clothes. An air eating away at the veritably being you were as you stepped into the shrouding scent.

I'd said the words a thousand times in my head, they were echoing around there, bouncing against each variation as my mind contended in anxiety. I watched as the cashier goggled with awaiting eyes, I only realized where I was as I met her eyes. Her lip was jiggling, petrified from the dread." Give me everything, everything on you, everything in the cash register, everything that is then." I could see as this old woman took in the words I said, her lips moving with the last words I'd uttered. The wrathfulness crawled on her face for a moment and faded as she saw the armament refocused at her cranium. I did not dare shake, I did not dare blench, this was a test of choices and if Marcus saw me slip, I'd be leaving this in a bag, to be set up three weeks from now In a wasteland of coca cola barrels, mammoths of McDonald's scrap; the recycled American Dream. I look back at the door for consolation," Give it over or I swear to god, we'll come back there for your son, and your hubby." Marcus was noway one to speak in mysteries, noway one to play with words. This woman stood down his cold dead eyes, and his armament drawn, sitting at his midriff.

Unwelcome recollections had ramified my grasp of reality, I only heard the enchantresses in a dream- suchlike haze, the bench bucketed with the expiring anxiety. The ground was stationary, the small haven I'd set up myself staying in came a glowing box of dread, guarding from the neon drenched road the bobby auto passed on. A horribly contorted beast mounted with a shrieking roar enough to stifle a high powered mutant, with a cushion bent to the crooked grin that would provoke a tadpole to sow legs, and a crooked faced man tending the light in the depths of the beast, as much along for the lift as whatever force drove it.

I felt the case shackled to my wrist grow heavier and heavier. The cracks blasted a light of felonious mischief. The beast crawled up the path and began to decelerate in front of the machine stop. I felt the haven fleetly drain of it's sense of safety, all that remained was the subtle drone of anxiety, so electric it was as though the air was carrying it's reach. The lights shone, and I came extremely apprehensive of my skin. Being I began to try and retire into it. My eyes closed I could still feel the dread course through my modes, like a quick shot of adrenaline blasting through my bloodstream, chancing me indeed the fewest breath recession, the mildest shiver. It was raining, I had not watched enough to know, I had not watched enough to concentrate. My head was buried in my sweater as I tried to hide from the posterity- ish regard of the tone- assured beat bobby who really was now gaping me down, from his high- powered mutant killing mammoth.

The recollections swamped with a revenge, the beasts roar had transferred a bad jolt into the recess' of my mind. I felt myself fight the studies, but as the fog crawled from the cells of the neon wasteland beyond.

"Please, please we need thi —" She began, where were my bases? Where was I now? My hand bound to this death loaded tool. I suppose I'd had not have noticed my hand at each, I suppose I'd be caught in the moment if I did not feel the grip in my hand. It felt white hot, it felt burning. Like I was not meant to be holding it at each, and perhaps, perhaps I wasn't, but it continued to gawk down the old woman in malignancy of that.

"Breath woman or we'll make sure you can't." I looked in a shocked bafflement, Marcus was the type of person who'd take a draft from a can of kerosene and also fight a terrier and look cool while doing it. My eyes cleaved in an nearly unwitting dismay until I began to see history, I suppose my eyes stayed a moment too long, there'd been commodity so bewitching of the neon" Open" sign that hung slanted against the door. The sterile fluorescent gleam felt divided by the gleam of the neon, guarding us from the absence beyond. A slow background music played as my regard sat on the sign, it came nearly disorienting, I could feel commodity I wouldn't want to see was about to be.

The rattle had been heard before, but the buzz entirely drowned out any of the other noises. Though I could not imagine I'd have had long to ignore it. The beast is sitting in front of me now, across the road. The sky cracked in nausea, and the auto's temptress blazoned violently. The darkness and distance contorted the faces in the auto. The neon reflected off of every billabong, depraved with each rain bullet. I'd have sworn the auto was filled with faceless men in black if I had not realized that what I was seeing was not real presently. The night was playing tricks on my eyes. Was I indeed then? Or was I in the store? Everything moves too presto, I slightly notice the sound of someone walk, a projectile blasts and I was certain where I was now.

“Oh god no!” I feel myself bruit . Turning in terror, I feel my arm fling back in front of the woman. I watch as she bounces against the wall, I did not feel my hand pull the detector, I did not feel it fire, I just looked to see how the neon shone that blood soaked shade that was ineffably different. My eyes danced by the doorway to see their sprat drooped over a cooler by the door, the shots pealed in our cognizance as we stood in terror, the room had not a sound. The calm that would really follow before I felt the corrosiveness begin to crawl up my esophagus.

I goggled down the auto now, reality came reeling in as the unwelcome memory faded to the reverse of my mind. All that remained was the anxiety, and the briefcase filled with the plutocrat from the store, and whatever differently Marcus had in there. For all I knew, I might be holding 3 pounds of fortified Nitroglycerin prepared in a lab long since busted in the lower town area. Thick globules of sweat dropped as I goggled the bobby down across the road. The auto innards light flashed his crooked face to a gentle weathered smile, some stager on the beat, opening the door. He closes the door behind him as he smiles looking back at a slow and unexciting day of work in his slice of Pleasantville. No need to ruin his Suburban safe-deposit box Haven tonight, so long as he’d leave me to sit.

I did not have to look as the sterile calm excavated into absolute insanity. Marcus got cropped and slammed against the door, the glass shattered as it landed by his burro as he hit the ground. I felt the shot hit my arm and spin me like a top. I look up in terror and I felt myself choke on the sick in my throat, I fired and felt as what sounded like hot sewage blast through my mouth and nostrils. I drop to my knees, the gun in my hand eventually dismounts and clatters on the bottom. I feel the sick work it’s way out of my body and in one last moment of ultimate defeat, feel absolute release. I slump onto my reverse and close my eyes under the sterile light. I raise my hand in an resentful attempt to block the light hanging ominously over, gaping me down, digging at this migraine that had worked its way over me as the anxiety erected. Wharf on my face as soon as I lifted it, I laid back and simply dozed off.

I do not flash back much of what would be next, I flash back the sounds I heard. It was like a defeated equivocation, the sound of commodity dragging and cussing as new problems would arise. I flash back being in and out of knowledge and wondering if I was awake at all. And, awake. Where was I? That question sat in the van of my mind for a moment before the hazy recollection of what had occurred the moments ahead. Let’s retrace our way, mammy riots” Stop.” Sprat drops, and also mama follows. Shotgun, and now I am then. Where was then? Where was Marcus?

“Marcus?!” I scream aimlessly.

“Yo--, ye — uhh.” I hear behind me. I look up to see him gushing blood from his side. I roll onto my side and press my knees against the carpet I laid on, to bottleneck to his bases.

“Marcus?! Wake up!!” He puffed a breath with a slightly open eye and left me with little stopgap of communication. At least verbal. Nothing is a better evidence of knowledge than a cold open win crossing your face,” Wake the hell up!!” A meaty poke would follow but he remained dazed.

“The coming bone‘s going to hurt like hell.” I said putting my arm behind his neck.

“Hey, hey man.” He started, I looked at his face and he’d a big stupid grin behind a brace of fliers he would seized from the rack beside him. I laugh in an nearly bittersweet defeat,” I am going to, I am going to--- uh." He tried to find the words, I suppose he was choosing them precisely, he wanted to know it'd be funny if it was the last bones he would say.

"I am going to freak out some coroners with how good I looked." I should not have laughed.

I suppose he was dead within a many further laboured breaths out from that, I was not sure, I did not have time to be. I dived for the cash register and bashed it until I could get it open. Snappily I loaded up the briefcase shackled to my wrist and made my way for the door. I walked past my friend's cadaver moment, and I ran for another block before I had time to let that Gomorrah by. Perhaps it had not registered ahead, but gaping down the bobby, standing by his auto now, I realized Marcus was most clearly a friend. And now he is lying in some general store in a pool of his own blood, wearing a brace of cheap crooked fliers . I suppose I'd have time for guilt or grief if it were not for the reason before all of this, clearing effects with Nico. That is why I was then at this machine stop, who I would be staying for.

I wouldn't dare meet eyes with the bobby, but I knew where he stood before I could do so much as club an eye at his presence. And he was walking towards me. My heart was in my throat, palpitating at a speed analogous to a wild boar carpeted in honey, sledding down a rugged hill. I could see him reaching for his fund, and felt the lack of weight on my midriff, where the dynamo had sat. He met eyes with me from behind his spectacles and smiled with his words, a healthy serving of tone- significance and condescension," You can not bomb then." I look up, blissfully ignorant of the mischief cigarette that hung to the corner of my mouth.

"What?" He goggled back unflinchingly.

"You, can't, bank, then. Understand?" I gawk back and fight the appetite to fish at my right side. As little attention as he paid to the crack the better.

"Yes officer." I said.

"Goodnight son," He responded, turning around snappily.

"Thank you, joe." I continued. He turned with a look of disgruntlement," Yes son, good night." He continued on, down past his auto and into a house of true suburban funk corral norms.

"God awful jagoff!" I murmured in disdain," Goddamned gormandizer." I continued.

I wondered if tonight was just a night that'd run on a little too long, perhaps it was just a terrible dream I had not escaped yet. Biding my time and suffering for it. Where was I now? I was not certain, I was not certain if I had a plan at all. I was not certain if Nico was coming, or if there was anything further I could do with this plutocrat that would amount to fill the void left by Marcus. Still important disdain I'd have had for him being in with Nico, I'd noway lost respect for him. I loved him, and chancing that was a hard thing to come by between a man and his prisoner. I could only hope the coming one Nico had transferred with me will have half the personality Marcus had, and two times further the immersion of lead. Perhaps it was luck I'd survived and he hadn't, perhaps a sick joke, but though I had no stopgap for the future I had seven hundred bones, and in the end that was further than I would really die for. No room for mercy, until the devil gets his pretenses.

Chapter No. 3: Forever and Always

The alley was dark as usual, the only sound the scuffling of rats and the soft breath. At the end of alley was a crooked drum chalet. It stank of rat poop and scrap, but I was used to it.

After all, it was my home.

Mother was staying for me. Her eyes were dull and empty, her lips cracked and slate. She was formerly beautiful, with lush, golden cinches, sparkling blue eyes, and pink lips always wide, smiling. She'd attend festivals and hops in dazing ball gowns, and dance with handsome youthful men who would propose to her by the end of the night. She turned down every single bone, until, eventually, she met the man who would soon come my father.

Also, he faded, along with the all the happy recollections.

A strong gust of wind blew right through our chalet, rattling the drum walls but not relatively tripping them over. My hair blew across my face, and I slobbered.

"Come then," Mother, croaked, slightly audible over the afterlife wind. I had vague recollections of her formerly melodious voice singing to me as I danced in my father's arms. However, perhaps we would still be doing that right at this moment, If only he had not faded into thin air.

I sat in my mama 's stage, and she trolled my hair before platting it with her quick, nimble fritters. That was the only thing my mama hadn't lost. That, and me. In fact, her fritters were what kept us living, each and every day. She'd mend clothes for the city residers, and they would pay her with the little food we demanded. She tied the end of my plat with a plain tie, and kissed the top of my head.

“I will get us out of then one day," She says." I promise."

I wake up to find Mother gone. Her bed is neatly made, and I notice that her only dress is missing from where it generally hangs on the reverse of a president. I know that she must have gone to city, but I can noway be too sure after what happed to Father. I pull on a fleece and walk the short distance to city. This beforehand in the morning is a quiet time, but there are occasional passers by that smile at me in acknowledgement.

Suddenly, a familiar squeal pierces the silent, afterlife air. Mother. I run through the thoroughfares, slow enough that I do not trip over my scuffed and torn shoes, but presto enough that the millions of studies contending through my mind do not cloud my thinking. mama is standing in the middle of the road, clinging commodity white. Its also that I realise it was a laugh of joy.

When I get to her, she's slightly recognizable. Colour has returned to her cheeks, and her eyes now have their sparkle back. She does not say a word, but rather thrusts the paper into my hand. I slump down onto a near demesne bench, and begin to read the letter.

My beautiful woman and son,

I'm sorry. For everything. The business trip to London was not anything like I anticipated. My father was dreadfully sick, and it was my duty to be with him in his final days. But it was my duty to be there for you, my girls, and I failed.

While in London, I transferred you letters every day. Either they noway got to you, or you have formerly forgotten me and moved on. I can not bear to return, for if you have moved on, nothing will ever be the same.

I've moved to Paris now, and have a beautiful big house and a thriving company. But what use is a lovely home if I can not partake it with the bones I love most?

Still, I would love for you to join me then, If you're reading this. Don't trouble yourself with aero plane tickets, I want to come and get you myself. I understand if you would rather stay in your birthplace, but I promise you that Paris is beautiful and if you consider coming, my broken heart will be healed.

Love,

Your hubby/ father, ever and always

I heaved and read the letter over and over again, just to make sure my mind wasn't going wild. When I looked at Mother, her eyes were shining with gashes.

“Honey," she said, pulling me close and bruiting in my observance." We are going to Paris."

Chapter No 4: Star of David

"I checked them out myself," Myra snapped. "Have you ever just considered that your boy is n't the angel you allowed he was? "

Stella took off her spectacles and set them on her office. "I suppose that we both need some perspective. Why do n't you take the rest of the autumn off? " Before I poke your stupid face. People like Devonte do n't change that presto, not without good reason.

Myra opened her mouth, but after she got a look at Stella's face she shut it again. Mutely she stalked to her office and recaptured her fleece and bag. She slammed the door behind her.

As soon as she was gone, Stella opened the brochure and looked at the filmland of the crime scene again. They were duplicates, and doubtless Clive, her family the operative, had broken a many rules when he transferred them to her — not that breaking rules had ever bothered him, not when he was five and not as a overgrown man nearing fifty and old enough to know more.

She touched the prints smoothly, also closed the brochure again. There was a unheroic sticky with a phone number on it and nothing additional Clive did n't have to put a name on it. Her little family knew she 'd see what he'd seen.

She picked up the phone and punched in the figures presto, not giving herself a chance for alternate studies.

The barracks were empty, leaving David's office silent and bleak. The boys were on redundancy with their colorful families for December.

His mercenaries specialized in live reclamation, which tended to be in and out stuff, a couple of weeks per job at the most. He did n't want to get involved in the argentine area of unsanctioned combat or out- and- out war where you killed people because someone told you to. In reclamation there were good guys and bad guys still — and if there were n't, he did n't take the job. Their character was similar that they had no trouble chancing jobs.

And unless all hell really broke loose, they always took December off to be with their families. David noway let them know how hard that made it for him.

Werewolves need their packs. Still, well, they knew about him and they filled that odd wolf- quip that demanded he have people to cover, If his pack was mortal. He could n't absorb a real pack, he abominated what he was too important.

He could n't bear to live with his own kind, but this worked as a cover and kept him centered. When his boys were then, when they had a job to do, he'd direction and purpose.

His grandsons had invited him for the family regale, but he 'd refused as he always did. He still saw his sons on a regular base. Both of them had served in his small band of mercenaries for a while, until the life lost its appeal or the pitfalls grew too great for men with growing families. But he stayed down at Christmas.

Restlessness had him pacing there were no plans to make, no wrongs to right. Eventually he uncorked the safe and pulled out a couple of the newer rifles. He demanded to put some time in with them anyway.

An hour of shooting staved off the restlessness, but only until he locked the ordnance up again. He 'd have to go for a run. When he voided his pockets in medication, he noticed he'd missed a call while he 'd been shooting. He glanced at the number, lowering when he did n't fete it. Utmost of his jobs came through an agent who knew better than to give out his cell number. Before he could decide if he wanted to return the call, his phone chimed again, a call from the same number.

"Christiansen, " he answered hastily.

There was a long silence. "Pop"

He closed his eyes and sank back in his president feeling his heart expand with nearly painful soberness as his wolf fought with the man who knew his son abominated him did n't want to see him, ever. She had been there when her mama failed.

"Stella?" He could n't imagine what it took to make her break nearly forty times of silence. "Are you each right? Is there commodity wrong? " Someone he could kill for her? A structure to blow up? Anything at all.

She swallowed. He could hear it over the line. He awaited for her to hang up. Rather, when she spoke again, her voice was brisk and the wavery pain that colored that first " pop " was gone as if it had noway been. " I was wondering if you would consider doing a favor for me. "

"What do you need? " He was proud that came out unevenly. Always better to know what you are getting into, he told himself. He wanted to tell her that she could ask him for anything — but he did n't want to scarify her.

"I run an agency that places foster kiddies, " she told him, as if he did n't know. As if her sisters had n't told her how he quizzed them to find out how she was doing and what she was over to. He hoped she noway set up out about herex-boyfriend who 'd turned snooper. He had n't killed that one, though his amenability to do so had made it easier to convert the man that he wanted to take up endless hearthstone in a different state.

"I know, " he said because it sounded like she demanded a response.

"There's commodity — " she dithered. " Look, this might not have been the stylish idea. "

He was losing her again. He'd to breathe deeply to keep the fear from his voice. " Why do n't you tell me about it anyway? Do you have commodity better to do? "

"I flash back that, " she said. " I flash back you doing that with mama. She 'd be hysterical, throwing dishes or books, and you 'd sit down and say, ' Why do n't you tell me about it? '"

Did she want to talk about her mama now? About the one time he 'd demanded to be calm and failed? He had n't known he was a werewolf until it was too late. Until after he 'd killed his woman and the nut she 'd taken while David had been fighting for God and country, both of whom had forgotten him. She 'd been staying until he came home to tell him that she was leaving it was a mistake she 'd had no time to lament. He, on the other hand, might have ever to lament it for her.

He noway spoke of it. Not to anyone. For Stella he 'd do it, but she knew the story anyway. She 'd been there.

"Do you want to talk about your mama ? " he asked, his voice carrying into a lower timbre; as it did when the wolf was close.

"No. Not that, " she said precipitously. " Nothing like that. I 'm sorry. This is n't a good idea. "

She was going to hang up. He drew on his hard- earned control and allowed presto.

Forty times as a huntsman and leader of men had given him a lot of practice reading between the lines. However, perhaps he could regain this, If he could put away the fact that she was his son.

She had told him she ran a foster agency like it was important to the rest of what she had to say.

"It's about your work " he asked, trying to figure out what a social worker would need with a werewolf. Oh. " Is there a — " His son preferred not to talk about werewolves, Clive had told him. So if there was commodity supernatural she was going to have to bring it up. " Is there someone bothering you? "

"No, " she said. " Nothing like that. It's one of my boys. "

Stella had noway married, noway had children of her own. Her family said it was because she had all the people to take care of that she could handle.

"One of the foster kiddies. "

"Devonte Parish. "

"He one of your special bones? " he asked. His Stella had noway seen a slapdash she had n't brought home, beast or human. utmost she 'd dusted off and transferred home with a mess and tapes as demanded but some of them she 'd kept.

She soughed. " Come and see him, would you? hereafter? "

"I 'll be there, " he promised. It would take him a many hours to set up authorization from the packs in her area trip was complicated for a werewolf. "presumably eventually in the autumn. This the number I can find you at? "

Rather of taking a hack from the field, he rented a auto. It might be harder to situate, but it would give them mobility and privacy. However, if she did n't want to bomb the peace pipe yet, also he did n't need it witnessed by a hack motorist, If his son only demanded this. A substantiation would make it harder for him to control himself — and his little girl noway demanded to see him out of control ever again.

He called her before setting out, and he could tell that she 'd had alternate and third studies.

"Look, " he eventually told her. " I 'm then now. perhaps we should go and talk to the boy. Where can I meet you? "

He'd have known her anywhere however he had n't, by her request, seen her since the night he 'd killed his woman. She'd been twelve and now she was a grown woman with tableware vestments running through her kinky black hair. The last time he 'd seen her she 'd been still a little rounded and soft as utmost children are and now there was n't an ounce of wimpiness in her. She was muscular and spare — like him.

It had been a long time, but he 'd noway have mistaken her for anyone differently she had his eyes and her mama 's face.

He 'd allowed you had to be bleeding someplace to hurt this poorly. The beast plodded within him, looking for an adversary. But he controlled and subdued it before he pulled the auto to the check and uncorked the automatic door.

She was wearing a brown hair suit that was several tones darker than the milk and coffee skin she'd gotten from her mama. His own skin was dark as the night and kept him safely hidden in the murk where he and people like him belonged.

She opened the auto door and got in. He awaited until she had fastened her seatbelt before pulling out from the check. Slush plashed out from under his tires, but it was only a commemorative. Once he was in the business lane the road was bare.

She did n't say anything for a long time, so he just drove. He'd no idea where he was going, but he figured she 'd tell him when she was ready. He kept his eyes on business to give her time to get a good look at him.

"You look youngish than I flash back , " she said eventually. " youngish than me. "

"I was thirty- five or thereabouts when I was Changed. Being a werewolf seems to settle physical age about twenty- five for utmost of us. " There it was out in the open and she could do with it as she pleased.

He could smell her fear of him spike and if he 'd really been twenty- five, he allowed he might have cried. Being this agitated was n't smart if you were a werewolf. He took a deep breath through his nose and tried to calm down — he 'd earned her sweat.

"Devonte wo n't talk to me or anyone differently, " she said, and also as if those words had been the key to the sluice she kept going. " I wish you could have seen him when I first met him. He was ten going on forty. He 'd just lost his grandmother, who had raised him. He looked me right in the eye, stuck his jaw out and told me that he demanded a home where he'd be clothed and fed so he could concentrate on academy. "

"Smart boy " he asked. She 'd started in the middle of the story he 'd forgotten that habit of hers until just now.

"Veritably smart. Quiet. But funny, too. " She made a sad sound, and her anguish overwhelmed her fear of him. " We screen the homes. We visit. But there's noway enough of us — and some of the horrible bones can put on a good show for a long time. It takes a while, too, before you get a sense for the bad ones. However, everything would have been fine, If he could have stayed with his first family. He stayed with them for six times. But this fall she suddenly got pregnant and her hubby got a job transfer... "

They 'd abandoned the boy like he was an old settee that was too awkward to move, David allowed. He felt a flash of wrathfulness for this boy he 'd noway met. He swallowed the emotion snappily; he could do that these days. For a while. He was going to have to take that run when he got back home.

"I was tied up in court cases and someone differently moved him to his coming family, " Stella continued, gaping at her hands, which were gripped on a manila brochure. " It should n't have been a problem. This was a family who formerly has fostered several children and Devonte was a good sprat, not the kind to give anyone problems. "

"But commodity happed? " he suggested.

"His foster mama says that he just went wild, throwing cabinetwork, breaking effects. When he hovered her, his foster father stepped in and knocked him out. Devonte's in the sanitarium with a broken wrist and two broken caricatures and he wo n't talk. "

"You do n't believe the foster family. "

She gave an indignant huff. " The Linnfords look likeMr. andMrs. Brady. She smiles and nods when he speaks and he's all charm and concern. " She raved again and spoke veritably precisely, " I would n't believe them if all they were doing was giving me the time of day. And I know Devonte. He just wants to get through academy and get a education so he can go to council and take care of himself. "

He jounced courteously. “ So why did you call me? ” He was willing to have a talk with the family, but he suspected if that was each she demanded it would have been a cold day in hell before she called him — she had her sisters for that.

“Because of the prints. ” She held up the brochure in assignation.

He'd to drive a couple of blocks before he set up a accessible parking place and pulled over, leaving the machine handling.

He pulled six prints off a clip that attached them to the reverse of the brochure she held and spread them out to look. Interest rose up and he wished he'd commodity further than prints. It clearly looked like further damage than one lone boy could do ten boys perhaps, if they had sledge hammers. The holes in the walls were commodity anyone could have done. The holes in the ten bottom ceiling, the administrative office on its side in three pieces and the antique oak president broken to slivers and missing a leg were more intriguing.

“The last time I saw commodity like that... ” Stella rumored.

It was presumably a good thing she could n't bring herself to finish that judgment . He'd to admit that all this scene was missing was blood and body corridor.

“How old is Devonte? ”

“Sixteen. ”

“Can you get me in to look at the damage? ”

“No, they had contractors in to fix it. ”

His eyebrows raised. “How long has it been”

“It was the twenty-first. Three days. ” She gestured a hand. “ I know. Contractors are generally a month stay at least, but plutocrat addresses. This joe has serious plutocrat. ”

That sounded wrong. “ also why are they taking in a foster sprat? ”

She looked him in the eye for the first time and jounced at him as if he ’d gotten commodity right. “ If I ’d been the one to vet them I ’d have smelled a rat right there. Rich folk do n’t want crossbred children who ’ve had it rough. Or if they do, they go to China or Romania and borrow babies to chirr over. They do n’t take in foster kiddies, not without an docket. But we ’re hopeless for foster homes... and it was n’t me who approved them. ”

“You said the boy would n’t talk. To you? Or to anybody? ”

“To anybody. He has n’t said a word since the incident. Wo n’t communicate at all. ”

David considered that, running through possibilities. “ Was anyone hurt except for the boy ”

“No. ”

“Would you mind if I went to see him now? ”

“Please.”

He followed her directions to the sanitarium. He situated the auto, but before he could open the door she seized his arm. The first time she touched him.

“Could he be a werewolf? ”

“Perhaps, ” he told her. “ That kind of damage... ”

“It looked like our house, ” she said, not looking at him, but not taking her hand off him moreover. “ Like our house that night. ”

Still, I misdoubt your Mr, “ If he was a werewolf. Linnford would have been about to knock him out without taking a lot of damage. perhaps Linnford is the werewolf. ” That would fit, utmost of the werewolves he knew, if they survived, ultimately came fat. Children were more delicate. perhaps that was why Linnford and his woman fostered children.

Stella jerked her chin up and down formerly. " That's what I allowed. That's it. Linnford might be a werewolf. Could you tell? "

His casket felt tight. How veritably stalwart of her she 'd called the only monster she knew to deal with the other monsters. It reminded him of how she 'd stood between him and the boys, guarding them the stylish that she could.

"Let me talk to Devonte, " he said trying to keep the scowl out of his voice with only moderate success. " also I can deal with Linnford."

The sanitarium corridors were decorated with symposium and green and red bulbs. Every time Christmas got more plastic and sounded further and further from the Xmases David had known as a child.

His son led him to the elevators without vacillation and changed nods with a many of the staff members who walked history. He abominated the way his children aged every time. abominated the tableware in their hair that was a constant memorial that ultimately time would take them all down from him.

She kept as important distance between them as she could in the elevator. As if he were a foreigner — or a monster. At least she was n't running from him screaming.

You ca n't live with bitterness. He knew that. Bitterness, like utmost unwelcome feelings, made the wolf restless. Restless wolves were dangerous. The nanny at the station just outside the elevator knew Stella, too, and saluted her by name.

"That Mr. Linnford was then asking after Devonte. I told him that he was n't allowed to visit yet. " She gave Stella a disappointed look, easily condemning her for puttingMr. Linnford to similar bother. " What a nice man he is, looking after that boy after what he did to them. "

She handed Stella a clipboard and gave David a mildly curious look. He gave her his most inoffensive smile and she smiled back before glancing down at the clipboard Stella had returned.

David could read it from where he stood. Stella Christiansen and guest. Well, he told himself, she could hardly write down that he was her father when she looked aged than he did.

"He may be a nice man, " Stella told the nanny with a thread of sword in her voice, " but you just keep him out until we know for sure what happed and why. "

She paraded off toward a set of doors where a bobby sat in front of a office, sitting on a rustic president, and reading a worn paperback dupe of Stephen King's Cujo. " Jorge, " she said.

"Stella, " he buzzed the door and let them through.

"He's in the secured sect, " she explained under her breath as she walked hastily down the hall. " Not that it's all that secure. Jorge should n't have let you through without checking your ID. "

Not that anyone would question his Stella, David allowed. Indeed as a little girl, people did what she told them to do. He was careful not to smile at her; she would n't understand it.

This part of the sanitarium smelled like blood, despair, and detergent. Indeed though utmost of the scents were old, a new wolf penned up in this terrain would beget a lot further excitement that he was seeing and a sixteen- time-old could only be a new wolf. Any youngish than that and they substantially did n't survive the Change. Anyway, he 'd have scented a wolf by now their first conclusion was right — Stella's boy was no werewolf.

"Any cameras in the apartments? " he asked in a low voice.

Her steady footfall broke. " No. That's still on the list of advised advancements for the future. "

"All right. No bone differently then? "

"Not right now, " she said. " This sanitarium is n't near gang home and they put the adult malefactors in a different section. " She entered one of the open doorways and he followed her in, shutting the door behind them.

It was n't a private room, but the first bed was empty. In the alternate bed was a boy gaping at the wall — there were no windows. He was beaten up a bit and had a cast on one hand. The other hand was attached to a sturdy rail that stuck out of the bed on the side nearest the wall with a locking nylon swatch — better than bind, he allowed, but not much. The boy did n't look up as they came by.

Perhaps it was the name, or perhaps the image that " foster sprat " brought to mind, but he 'd anticipated Devonte to be black. rather, the boy looked as if someone had taken half a dozen races and shook them up — Eurasian races, however, not from the Dark Continent. There was Native American or Oriental in the corners of his eyes and he supposed that nose could be Jewish or Italian. His skin looked as if he'd a deep suntan, but this time of time it was more likely the color was his own Mexican, Greek or indeed Indian.

Not that it signified. He 'd set up that the times were sluggishly completing the job that Vietnam had begun — race or religion signified veritably little to him presently. But indeed if it had signified... Stella had asked him for help.

Stella glanced at her father. She did n't know him, did n't know if he 'd see through Devonte's recalcitrant sulkiness to the fear under. His vacant face and upright military bearing gave her no indication. She could read people, but she did n't know her father presently, had n't seen him since... that night. Watching him made her uncomfortable, so she turned her attention to the other person in the room.

"Hey, sprat. "

Devonte kept his aspect on the wall.

"I brought someone to see you. "

Her father, after a keen look at the boy, lifted his head and smelled in air through his nose hard enough she could hear it.

"Where are the clothes he was wearing when they brought him in? " he asked.

That drew Devonte's attention and satisfaction at his response braked her answer. Her father's eye fell on the locker and he stalked to it and opened the door. He took out the clear plastic bag of clothes and said, with studied indifference, " Linnford was then asking about you moment. "

Devonte went still as a mouse.

Stella did n't know where this was going, but pitched in to help. " The police informed me that Linnford's decided not press assault charges. They should move you to a room with a view soon. I 'm listed for a meeting hereafter morning to decide what happens to you when you get out of then. "

Devonte opened his mouth, but also closed it intensively.

Her father scented at the bag, also said vocally, " Why do your clothes smell like shark, boy "

Devonte jumped, the whites of his eyes showing all the way round his irises. His mouth opened and this time Stella allowed it might really be an incapability to speak that kept him quiet. She was choking a bit on " shark " herself. But she would n't have believed in werewolves either, she supposed, if her father were n't one.

"I did n't introduce you, " she muttered. " Devonte, this is my father, I called him when I saw the crime scene prints. He's a werewolf. " If he was having shark problems, perhaps a werewolf would look good.

The sad blue-argentine president with the ripped naughahyde seat that had been sitting next to Devonte's bed zipped past her and slung itself at her father — who caught it and gave the boy a curious halfsmile. " Oh I go you surprised it, did n't you? Wizards are n't exactly common. "

"Wizard? " Stella grassed regrettably.

Her father's smile widened just a little — a smile she flashed back from her nonage when she or one of her sisters had done commodity particularly clever. This bone was aimed at Devonte.

He moved the president gently between his hands. " A witch's power centers on bodies and minds, meat and blood. A wizard has power over the physical — " The empty bed slammed into the wall with the open locker, bending the door and cracking the drywall. Her father was safely in front of it and delinquently she realized he must have jumped over it.

He still had the president and his smile had grown to a wide, white grin. " veritably nice, boy. But I 'm not your adversary. " He glanced up at the timepiece on the wall and shook his head.

"Someone ought to reset that thing. Do you know what time it is "

No more cabinetwork moved. Her father made a show of taking out his cell phone and looking at it. " Six- thirty. It's dark outside formerly. How poorly did you hurt it with that president I saw in the print? "

Devonte was breathing hard, but Stella controlled her appetite to go to him. Her father, hopefully, knew what he was doing. She fiddled, though she was wearing her favorite hair suit and the sanitarium was relatively warm. How important of the stories she had heard about vultures was true?

Devonte released a breath. "Not poorly enough. "

On the tails of Devonte's reply, her father asked, "Who tutored you not to talk at each, if you have a secret to keep? "

"My grandmother. Her mama survived Dachau because the American colors came just in time and because she kept her mouth shut when the Nazis wanted information. "

Her father's face softened. "Tough woman. Was she the Gypsy? Utmost wizards have at least a little vagabond blood. "

Devonte signed, rubbed his hands over his face hard. She honored the gesture from a hundred different kiddies he was trying not to cry. " Stella said you 're a werewolf. "

Her father cocked his head as if he were importing commodity. "Stella does n't lie. " suddenly he projected Stella with his eyes. " I do n't know if we 'll have a shark calling tonight — it depends upon how poorly Devonte hurt it. "

"Her, " said Devonte. " It was her. "

Still looking at Stella, her father corrected himself. “Her. She must have been enough poorly injured if she has n’t come then formerly. And it presumably means we ’re lucky and she's alone. If there were others they ’d have come history or the day before they ca n’t go to let Devonte live with what he knows about them. vultures have n’t survived as long as they've by leaving substantiations. ”

“No one would have believed me, ” Devonte said. “ They ’d have locked me up ever. ”

That made her father release her from the grip of his aspect

as he concentrated his attention on Devonte. The boy uncurled under the impact — Stella knew exactly how he felt.

“Is that what Linnford told you when his neighbors came running to see why there was so important noise? ” her father asked gently. “ upmarket apartment residers are n’t nearly as likely to ignore odd sounds. Is that why you threw around so important cabinetwork? That was smart, boy. ”

Devonte was seesawing his head and he uncurled a little more at her father’s praise.

“Coming time a shark attacks you and you do n’t manage to kill it, however, you roar it to the world. You may end up seeing a psychologist for the rest of your life but the vultures will stay as far from you as they can. However, you tell your story to the journals, If she does n’t come tonight. ” Her father glanced at Stella and she jounced.

“I know a couple of journalists, ” she said. “‘ Boy Claims He Was Attacked by Vampire ’ ought to vend enough papers to justify a caption or two. ”

“Each right also, ” her father returned his attention to her. “ I need you to go out and find some wood for us a president, a table, commodity we can make stakes out of. ”

“Holy water? ” asked Devonte. “ They might have a tabernacle then. ”

“Smart, ” said her father. “ But from what I ’ve heard it does n’t do enough damage to be worth running it down. Go now, Stella — and be careful. ”

She nearly accredited him, but she did n’t trust him enough to tease. He saw it, nearly smiled and also turned back to Devonte. “And you ’re going to tell me everything you know about this shark. ”

Stella glanced in the room next to Devonte’s, but, like his, it was decorated in early naughahyde and essence no wood to be set up. She did n’t bother checking any further but hastened to the security door — and read the note on the door.

“No, joe. She lived with them — they told me she was Linnford’s family. ” Devonte stopped talking when she came back.

“Jorge’s been called down, he ’ll be back in a many twinkles. ”

Her father considered that. “ I suppose the show’s on. No rustic chairpersons? ”

“All the apartments in this sect are like this bone. ”

“Without an effective armament, I ’ll get a better chance at her as a wolf also as a mortal. It means I ca n’t talk to you though — and it'll take a while to change back, perhaps a couple of hours. ” He looked down, and in an adult interpretation of Devonte’s earlier gesture, rubbed his face tiredly. She heard the scrape of whisker on skin. “ I control the wolf now and have for a long time. ”

He was upset about her.

“It’s all right, ” she told him. He gave her the same kind of keen examination he ’d given Devonte before and she wondered what information he was drawing from it. Could he tell how spooked she was?

His face softened. " You 'll do, my star. "

She 'd forgotten that he used to call her that — abominated the way it tensed her throat. " Should I call Clive and Steve "

"Not for a shark, " he told her. " All that will do is up the body count. To that end, we 'll stay then and stay an insulation ward is as good a place to face her as any. However, and the guard's departing is n't the morning of her attack if she does n't come tonight, we get all of us into the safety of someone's home, If I 'm wrong. also I 'll call in a many favors and my musketeers and I can take care of her nearly there are n't any civilians to be hurt. "

He looked around with apparent dissatisfaction.

"What are you looking for? " Devonte asked so she did n't have to.

"A place to hide. " also he looked up and smiled at the dropped ceiling.

"Those panels wo n't support your weight, " she advised him.

"No, but this is a sanitarium and this is the old sect. I go they've a string graduation for their computer and electric lines... " As he spoke, he 'd hopped on the empty bed and pushed up a ceiling panel to take a look.

"What's a string graduation? " Stella asked.

"In this case, it's a sturdy aluminum track attached to the oak ray with stout tackle. " He sounded pleased as he replaced the ceiling panel he 'd taken out. " I could hide a couple of people over then if I had to. "

He was a mercenary, she flashed back, and wondered how numerous times he 'd hidden on top of string graduations.

He moved the empty bed down from the wall and climbed on it again and removed a different panel. "Do you suppose you can get this panel back where it belongs after I get up then, boy"

"Sure." Devonte sounded completely pleased. If anyone differently had called him " boy " he 'd have been bristling. He was formerly well on the way to a big case of idol deification, just like the one she 'd had.

"Stella. " Her father took off his red blarney shirt and laid it on the empty bed behind him.

"When this is over, you call Clive, tell him everything and he 'll arrange a remittal. He knows who to call for help with it. It's safer for everyone if people do n't believe in vultures and werewolves. Leaving bodies makes it kind of hard to deny. "

"I 'll call him. "

Without his shirt to cover him, she could see there was no wimpiness in him. A many scars showed up slate on his dark skin. She 'd forgotten how dark he was, like ebony.

As he hulled off his sky-blue undershirt he said, with a touch of humor, " if you do n't want to see further of your father than any son ever should, you need to turn your reverse. " And she realized she 'd been gaping at him.

Devonte made an odd noise he was laughing. There was a miserliness to the sound and she knew he was spooked and agitated to see what it looked like when a man changed into a werewolf. For some reason she felt her own mouth stretch into a nervous grin she let Devonte see just before she did as her father advised her and turned her back.

David did n't like changing in front of anyone. He was n't exactly vulnerable but it made the wolf edgy and if someone decided to get stalwart and approach too nearly.... well, the wolf would feel hovered , like a snake slipping its skin.

So to the boy he said still, "Watching is fine. But stay for a bit if you want to touch... " He'd a study. " Stella, if she sends the Linnfords in first, I 'll do my stylish to stay retired. I can take a shark... " Honesty forced him to continue. "Perhaps I can take a shark, but only with surprise on my side. Her mortal pets, if they're still mortal enough to walk in daylight, are still too mortal to descry me. Do n't let them take Devonte out of this room. "

He tried to flash back everything he knew about vultures. Once he changed, it would be too late to talk. " Do n't look in the shark's eyes, do n't let her touch you. Unless you're really a religionist, do n't plan on crosses helping you out. When I attack, do n't try and help, just keep out of it so I do n't have to worry about you. "

Wishing they had a rustic stake, he knelt on the bottom and allowed himself to change. Calling the wolf was easy, it knew there was a fight to be had, blood to be exfoliate, and in its appetite it rushed the change as if called by the moon herself.

He noway flashed back exactly how bad it was going to hurt. His mama had formerly told him that parturition was like that for women. That if they flashed back how bad it was, they would warrant the courage to face the coming time.

But he did flash back it was always worse than he anticipated, and that ever helped him bear it.

The glacial, icy pain slid over his bones while fire threaded through his muscles, reshaping, reorganizing and altering what was there to suit itself. Experience kept him from making noise — it was one of the first effects he learned how to control his instincts and keep the howls, the growls, and the gripes outside and bury them in silence. Noise can attract unwanted attention.

His lungs labored to give oxygen as adrenaline forced his heart to beat too presto. His face pained as teeth came fangs and his jaw extended with cheekbones. His sight blurred and also stoned with a raptorial clarity that allowed him to see prey and adversary likewise no matter what murk they tried to hide in.

"Cool," said someone. Devonte. He who was- to-be-guarded.

Someone moved and it attracted his attention. Her terror swamped his senses like incense.

Prey. He liked it when they ran.

Also she lifted her chin and he saw a alternate image, superimposed over the first. A child standing between him and two lower children, her chin protruding out as she lifted up a baseball club in wordless defiance that spoke louder than the her terror and the blood.

Not prey. Not prey. His. His star.

It was each right also. She could see his pain — she had earned that right. And together they would stop the monster from eating the boy.

For the first many twinkles after the change, he substantially allowed like the wolf, but as the pain subsided he settled back into control. He shook off the last of unwelcome tingles with the same restraint he used to set aside the desire to snarl at the boy who reached out with a hand... only to haul back, caught by the swatch on his wrist.

David hopped on to the bed and snapped through the ballistic nylon that attached Devonte's cuff to the rail and awaited while the boy patted him tentatively with all the seductiveness of a person touching a barracuda.

"That 'll be a little hard to explain, " said Stella.

He looked at her and she squinched... also jerked up her chin and met his eyes. " What if the Linnfords ask about the restraint? "

It had been the wolf's response to seeing the boy he was supposed to cover tied up like a bad canine, not the man's.

"They'ven't been then, " said Devonte. " Unless they spend a lot of time in sanitarium captivity, they wo n't know it was supposed to be there. I 'll cover the cuff on my wrist with the mask. "

Stella jounced her head courteously. "All right. And if effects get bad, at least this way you can run. He's right, it's better if the restraint is out. "

David let them work it out. He launched himself off Devonte's bed and onto the other — forgetting that Devonte was formerly hurt until he heard the boy's indrawn breath. David was still partial- operating on wolf instincts, which was n't veritably helpful when fighting vultures. He demanded to be allowing.

Perhaps it had only been the suddenness of his movement however because the boy made the same sound when David hopped through the nearly- too-narrow opening in the ceiling and onto the track in the plenum space between the original fourteen- bottom ceiling and false panels fitted into the flimsy hangers that kept them place. The track moaned a little under his unforeseen weight, but it did n't bend.

"My father always told us that no bone ever looks up for their adversary, " Stella said after a moment. " Can you replace the panel? If you ca n't I — "

The panel he 'd moved slid back into place with further force than necessary and cracked down the middle.

"Damn it. "

"Do n't worry, no bone will notice. There are a couple of broken panels over there. "

She could n't see any sign that her father was hiding in the ceiling except for the bed. She seized it by the headboard and dragged it back to its original position, also she did the same with the president.

She'd forgotten how emotional the wolf was... nearly beautiful the perfect killing machine covered with four- inch-deep, redgold fur. She had n't flashed back the black that sloped his cognizance and girdled his eyes like Egyptian camouflage.

Still, I 'll see what I can do with the wall, " said Devonte, " If you 'll get back. " occasionally I can fix effects as well as move them. "

That gave her a little pause, but she set up that wizards were n't as shocking as werewolves and vultures. She considered his offer, also shook her head.

"No. They formerly know what you are. " She gathered her father's clothes from the counterpane and folded them neatly. Also she stockpiled them — and the plastic bag with Devonte's clothes — into the locker. "Just leave the wall. We only need to hide the werewolf from them, and you might need all the power you 've got to help with the shark. "

Devonte jounced.

"Right also. " She took a deep breath and picked up her catch all bag from the bottom where she'd set it.

Her sisters had made fun of her pocketbooks until she 'd used one to take out a bushwhacker. She 'd been lucky — it had been laden with a brace of three- pound weights she 'd been transporting from home to work but she 'd noway admitted that to her sisters.

latterly they 'd given her Mace, karate assignments, and quit chivying her about the size of her bag.

Exhuming a trip- sized game board from its depths she said, " How about some checkers?"

Five hard- won games latterly she decided the shark either was n't coming tonight, or she was staying for Stella to go down. She jumped three of Devonte's checkers and there was a quiet knock on the door. She turned to look as Jorge, the bobby who 'd gotten babysitting duty moment, stuck his head in.

"Sorry to leave you stuck then. "

"No problem. Just beating a poor helpless child at checkers."

She awaited for him to respond with commodity funny — Jorge was quick on his bases. But his face just stayed... not blank precisely, but neutral.

"They need you down in pediatrics, now. Looks like a case of child abuse and Doc Gonzales wants you to talk to the little girl. "

She could n't help the instincts that brought her to her bases, but those same instincts were screaming that there was commodity wrong with Jorge.

Between her job and having a family on the force, she 'd gotten to know some of the bobbies enough well. Nothing bothered Jorge like a child who 'd been hurt. She 'd seen him cry like a baby when he talked about a auto wreck where the child had n't survived. But he 'd passed this communication along to her with all the passion of a sanitarium switchboard driver.

In the pictures, vultures could make people do what they wanted them to — she could n't flash back if the people were permanently damaged. substantially, she was hysterical , they just failed.

She glanced down at her watch and shook her head. " You know my rules, " she said. " It's after six and I 'm off shift. "

Her rules were a standing joke with her sisters and their musketeers — a serious joke. She 'd seen too numerous people burn out from the stress of her job. So she 'd made a list of rules she had to follow, and they 'd kept her stable so far. One of her rules was that from eight in the morning until six in the evening she was on the job, outside of those hours she did her stylish to have a real life. She was breaking it now, with Devonte.

Rather of calling her on it, Jorge just reused her reply and eventually jounced. " All right. I 'll tell them. "

He did n't close the door when he left. She went to the doorway and watched him walk mechanically down the hall and through the security door, which he 'd left open. veritably unlike him to leave a security door open, but he closed it behind him.

" That was the shark's exploit was n't it? " she asked, looking up.

The soft scowl that eased through the ceiling was ever reassuring however she had n't forgotten his reservations about how well he 'd do against a shark.

She went back to Devonte's bed and made her move on the board. Out in the hall the security door opened again, and someone wearing high heels click- clicked hastily down the hall.

Stella took a deep breath, settled back on the end of the bed and told Devonte, " Your turn."

He looked at the board, but she saw his hand shake as whoever it was in the hallway closed in on them.

"King me, " he said in a fair approximation of triumph.

The steps stopped in the doorway. Devonte looked over her shoulder and his face went slack with fear. Stella gobbled and took her first look.

She 'd allowed a shark would be youthful, like her father. Was n't that the myth? But this woman had argentine hair and wrinkles under her eyes and in the soft, white skin of her neck. She was dressed in a professionally- acclimatized wine- colored suit. She wore a diamond choker around her aging neck, and diamond- and- plum earrings.

"Well, " said Stella, " No bone is going to suppose you look like a cuddly grandma. "

The woman laughed, her face lighting up with a cheer so genuine that Stella allowed she might have liked her if only the horselaugh did n't showcase her fangs. " The boy talked, did he? I allowed for sure he 'd hold his lingo, if only to keep his own secrets. Either that or broadcast it to the world, and also you and I would n't be in this position. "

She gave Stella a kindly smile that showed off a charmingly mismatched brace of dimples. "I'm sorry you had to be involved. I tried to get you out of it. "

But Stella had been dealing with people a long time, she could smell a fake a afar down. The horselaugh had been real, but the kind concern clearly was n't.

"Separating your prey, " Stella said. She demanded to get the shark into the room where her father could drop on top of her, but how?

The shark displayed her fangs and dimples again. " More accessible and easier to keep the noise down, " she allowed. " But not really necessary. Not indeed if you're a — " she took a deep breath, " — werewolf. "

The news did n't feel to bother her. Stella fought off the feeling that her father was going to beover-matched. He 'd been a dogface and also a mercenary, training his own sons and also grandsons. Surely he knew what he was doing.

"Hah, " sniggered Devonte in classic adolescent misprision. " You are n't so tough. I nearly killed you all by myself. "

The shark sniggered right back and, on her, the expression made the hair on the reverse of Stella's neck stand up and take notice. " You were a mistake, boy. One I intend to clear up."

David squinched motionless, staying for the sound of the shark's voice to indicate she had moved underneath him.

Tolerance, tolerance, he counseled himself, but he should have been counseling someone differently.

Still, they drove Devonte into action, If the shark's theatrics spooked Stella. The bed he tried to smash her father with rattled across the bottom. He must have tired himself out with his earlier enchantment because it was traveling only half as presto as it had when he had tried to drive her father through the wall.

The shark had no trouble grabbing it... or throwing it through the cataplasm wall and into the hallway where it crashed on its side, tossing bus, coverlet, mattress and pieces of the arcana that distinguished it from a normal bed.

She was so busy impressing them with her inconceivable gawk reproduction, she did n't see the old blue-argentine president. It hit her exactly in the reverse, driving her directly under the panel Devonte had cracked.

“Now,” rumored Stella diving toward the hole the shark had made in the wall, hoping that would be out of the way.

Indeed though Devonte’s president had knocked the shark to her knees, Stella’s stir drew her attention. The thing was presto, and she dived for Stella in the same stir she used to rise. Also the roof fell on top of her, the roof and a quietly snarling redgold wolf with claws and fangs that made the shark’s look like toys.

For a moment, she was twelve again, watching the monster dig those long claws into her mama’s nut and she set in horror. The woman looked frail beneath the huge wolf's bulk — until she pulled her legs under him and threw him into the external wall, the one made of cinder blocks and not cataplasm.

With an inhuman howl, the shark bounded upon her father. She looked nothing like the elegant woman who had walked into the room. In the brief regard she ’d had of her face, Stella saw commodity terrible... wrong.

“Stella, behind you!” Devonte yelled, hopping of the bed, his good arm around his caricatures.

She had n’t been paying attention to anything except the shark. Devonte’s warning came just a little late and someone seized her by the arm and jerked her roughly around — Linnford. Gone was the civic smile and GQ posture; his face was lit with fanaticism and madness. He'd a cutter in the hand that was n’t holding her. She replied without allowing, twisting so his thrust went past her tummy, slicing though fabric but not skin.

Commodity buzzed between them, hitting him in the casket and knocking him back to the bottom. He jerked and spasmed like a skewered frog in a film she ’d formerly had to watch in council. The president sat on top of him, balanced on one fraudulent leg, the other three appearing to hang in the air.

It took a moment for her to duly understand what she was seeing. The fraudulent president leg was stuck into his ribcage, just to the left wing of his sternum. Blood began sticking out like a lurid root.

“Honey? ” Hannah Linnford stood in the doorway. Like Stella, she sounded to be having trouble understanding what she was seeing.

Murmuring, “ Does no bone flash back to shut the security doors? ” Stella pulled themini-canister of Mace her youthful family had given her after the swiping incident out of her fund and scattered it in the other woman’s face.

If she had been holding Linnford’s cutter she could have mirthfully driven it through Hannah’s neck These people had taken one of her kiddies and tried to feed him to a shark.

Thinking of her kiddies made Stella look for Devonte.

He was leaning against the wall a many bases from his bed, gaping at Linnford and his expression centered Stella because he demanded her. She ran to him and dragged him to the far corner of the room, down from the fighting monsters, but too close to the Linnfords. Once she had him where she wanted him, she did her stylish to block his view of Linnford’s dying body. However, Linnford might survive but she felt no drive to do it, If she could get medical help soon enough. Let him rot.

Mace can in hand, she kept a rainfall eye on the woman screaming on the bottom, but utmost of her attention was on the fight her father was losing.

They fought like a brace of pussycats, coming together clawing and smelling, nearly too fast for her eyes to concentrate on, also, for no reason she could see, they would retreat.

After a many seconds of gaping at each other, they would go at it again. Unlike pussycats, they were eerily silent.

The shark is precisely arranged hair was fallen, covering her face, but not disguising her spangling... no, glowing red eyes. Her arm flashed out in a jerky movement that was so quick Stella nearly missed it — and the wolf twitched down with another crack that dropped blood the shark was still nearly untouched.

The two monsters backed down from each other and the shark licked her fritters.

"You taste so good, wolf, " she said. " I ca n't stay until I can sink my fangs through your skin and stink that agreeableness sot. "

Stella scattered Hannah in the face again. also she hauled Devonte out the door and down from the shark, making regrettably little allowance for his broken caricatures. Dead was worse than in pain.

It is working, David allowed, watching the shark master his blood off her fritters. Though he was substantially concentrated on the shark, he noticed when Stella took the boy out of the room. Good for her. With the shark's pets then, one dead and one incapacitated, she should n't have trouble getting out. He hoped she took Devonte to her home — or any home where they would be safe. also he put them out of his mind and concentrated on the battle at hand.

He had met a shark or two, but noway fought one ahead. He 'd heard that some of them had a strange response to werewolf blood. She sounded to be one of them.

He could only hope that her blood lust would make her stupid. He 'd heard that vultures could n't feed from the dead. However, he might be in trouble, If it was n't true.

He awaited for her to come at him again and this time he stepped into her fist, falling limply at her bases. She hit him hard, he felt the bone in his jaw creak, so the limp fall was n't hard to fake. He 'd stay until she started feeding, and the residual dizziness from her blow left, also he 'd take her.

She fell on him and he awaited for her fangs to dig in. rather she jerked a couple of times and also lay still. She was n't breathing and her heart was n't beating but she 'd been like that when she walked into the room.

"Pop"

Stella was supposed to be safely down.

He rose with a roar, making an audible sound for the first time so the shark would pay attention to him and leave his son alone. But the woman's body rolled easily off of him and lay on the bottom — two rustic president legs stuck through her reverse.

"Are you each right? Jorge left the security door open, I knew it when the Linnfords came in. We broke the legs off Jorge's president and used whatever he used to toss the cabinetwork around to drive them into her reverse. "

The dogface in him claimed on a full and quick check of the room. Linnford was dead, the abused president was the egregious cause of death. A woman, presumably his woman, blubbed roughly, her face pressed into Linnford's arm a possible trouble. Stella and Devonte were standing way too close to the shark.

They 'd killed her.

For a moment he felt a swell of pride. Stella did n't have an ounce of quit in her whole body. She and the boy had managed to take advantage of the distraction he 'd arranged before he could.

“Everyone was gone, Jorge and everyone ” He looked at the triumph in Stella’s face, not relatively retired by her solicitude for her musketeers.

She allowed the shark was finished, but wood through the heart did n’t always keep the undead down.

“Are you each right? ” Stella asked. And also when he just goggled at her, “pop”

He ’d come then hoping to play idol, he knew, hoping to mend what could n’t be mended. But the only part for him was that of monster, because that was the only thing he was.

He pulled the distance off the bed and ripped it with a claw, also tossed it toward Linnford’s blubbing woman. Stella took the hint and she and Davonte made a rope of feathers out of it and tied her up.

While they were working at that, he walked sluggishly over to the shark. Stella had called him pop tonight, further than formerly. He ’d try to hold on to that and forget the rest.

He growled at the shark her fault that he'd lose his son a alternate time. also he snapped his teeth through her chine. The meat of her was tougher than it should have been, tougher than jerky and bad tasting to charge. His jaw hurt from the megahit he ’d taken as he set his teeth and put some muscle into separating her head from her body.

When he was finished, the boy was losing his last mess in the corner, an arm wrapped around his caricatures. Throwing up with broken caricatures smelled he knew all about that. Linnford’s woman was secured. Stella had a hand over her mouth as if to help herself from imitating Devonte. When she pulled her eyes down from the shark’s disassociated head and looked at him, he saw horror.

He felt the blood trickling from his jaws and could n’t face her any longer. Could n’t stay while horror turned to fear of him. He did n’t look at his son again as he ran down for the first time in his long life.

When he could, he changed back to mortal at the home of the original werewolf pack. They let him shower, and gave him a brace of sweats — the universal answer to the common problem of changing back to mortal and not having clothes to put back on.

He called his oldest son to make sure that Stella had called him and that he'd handled the remittal. She had flashed back , and Clive was pacing with his usual thoroughness.

Linnford was about to have a terrible auto wreck. The shark’s body, both corridor of it, were listed for immediate incineration. The biggest problem was what to do with Linnford’s woman. For the moment she sounded to be too traumatized to talk. perhaps the shark’s death had broken her — or perhaps she ’d come around. Either way, she ’d need help, discreet help from people who knew how to tell the difference between the victim of a shark and a speed and would treat her consequently.

David made a many calls, and got the number of a veritably private sanitorium run by a small, veritably secret government agency. The price was n’t bad — each he'd to do was deliver some missionary who was related to a high- position politician. The fool had managed to get abducted with his woman and two youthful children. David’s platoon would still get paid, and he ’d presumably have taken the assignment anyway.

By the time he called Clive back, his sons had located a many missing sanitarium labor force and the bobby who ’d been guarding the door. David heard the relief in Clive’s voice Jorge was supposedly a friend. None of the recovered people sounded to be hurt, though they had no idea why they were each in the basement.

David hung up and turned off his cell phone. Accepting the offer of a bedroom from the pack nascence, David took his tired body to bed and slept.

Christmas day was coming to a close when David drove his reimbursement to his son's house — musketeers had picked it up from the sanitarium for him.

Red and green lights covered every backcountry and rail as well as girding all the windows. Knee-high delicacy canes lined the walk.

There were buses at his son's house. David lowered at them and checked his new watch. He was coming over at the right time. He 'd made it clear that he did n't want to intrude — which was understood to mean that he would n't come when Stella was likely to be there.

He'd formerly have been on a flight home, except that he did n't know how to communicate Devonte. He tapped the envelope against his leg and wondered why he 'd picked up a Christmas card rather of just handing over his business card. Below his contact information he'd made Devonte an open job offer beginning as soon as Devonte was eighteen. David could suppose of a thousand ways a wizard would be of use to a small group of mercenaries.

Of course, after watching David tear up the shark's body, Devonte presumably would n't be interested, so further to the point was the name and phone number on the other side of the card. Both belonged to a wizard who was willing to take on a pupil; the original nascence had given it to him.

Clive had promised to give it to Devonte.

David had to search under the giant wreath on the door for the bell. As he awaited, he noticed that he could hear a lot of people outside, and indeed through the door he smelled the lemon.

He took a step back, but the door was formerly opening.

Stella stood in the doorway. Over her shoulder, he could see the whole family running around preparing the table for Christmas regale. Devonte was sitting on the settee reading to one of the toddlers that sounded to be everywhere. Clive leaned against the fireplace and met David's aspect. He lifted a glass of wine and belted it, smiling slyly.

David took another step back and opened his mouth to apologize to Stella... just as her face lit with her mama's smile. She stepped out onto the veranda and wrapped her arms around him.

"Merry Christmas, pop," she said. "I hope you like lemon."

Chapter No. 5: The Judgement

The court came to order and the Judge entered, not with the treble call of bugles or the roll of cans, but in silence and alone. His men at- arms were outdoors, breastplates under their tunics as always, brands at the ready, and phylacteries at their necks. Since this was a trial for murder by necromancy, maybe this last was the most important.

The Judge took his seat in the high, sculpted president, behind the ancient bench with its poems and symbols so dark with use they were nearly insolvable to read. He was a altitudinous man, but beneath his substantial blankets his body might have been any shape.

The Prosecutor awaited as everyone settled in his or her places. There was a big crowd moment, drawn by fear and excitement. He was intolerant to begin, and he could see that the Judge was also. It was clear in his hard, clever face, indeed, though he made no move to quicken the ushers. Maybe he liked seeing them in their black blankets, moving like murk, or monuments of doom.

The Procurator shifted his weight from one bottom to the other. He knew he'd win. It was a simple case of a woman who had cheated after her family- in- law. When he'd rejected her, forcing her to face the verity of his fidelity to his woman, she had avenged herself by casting a spell which had caused his death. Murder by necromancy could hardly be clearer. The trial was really just to demonstrate that justice was done. To begin with he'd been intolerant with the waste of time and the cost of it, until he'd appreciated the truculent effect on other women who might be tempted to such a thing. This new Judge was right to do, and intimately. Regrettably, it was a necessary performance. These days too numerous people were ignorant of the reality of dark powers. They demanded reminding of justice, and where it was traduced, of discipline.

At last they were settled, and the Chief Usher read out the charge. The indicted denied it. Her voice might typically be affable, her diction was beautiful, but now she was strained with fear. Good. So she should be. The Prosecutor looked at her curiously. She was relatively altitudinous. And slender. The weight of the chains on her must hurt. She wasn't beautiful, there was too important passion in her face. It was clever and willful, maybe what should be anticipated in one who turned to witchery.

He stood up. "My fellow citizens! " His voice chimed around the room. He surveyed them. After all, this was for their benefit, or it could have been done intimately. He was interested to see that there were as numerous women then as men. Some were in fine dresses of rich fabric decorated with embroidery, the heavy cinctures around their middles were speckled with gems, their hair pleated with lists. Others wore plain browns and courtesans, hair tied back with scarves, as if recently come in from some form of work.

The men too were of every variety, knights- at- arms, clerks in brown jerkins with essay-stained fritters, scholars and crafters with calloused hands. He saw at least one apothecary — now there was an art which at times verged too close to the conjurers ! And of course there were numerous growers and labourers. The dead man had been a planter, a rich bone.

He called his first substantiation, Stroban, the dead man's father. Stroban moved forward from the frontal bench and into the Square of Testimony, uncurling his shoulders with an trouble. Grief had progressed him in a many terrible days. His face was blanched of color, his slate hair sounded thinner, drawn across his cranium like an shy protection. He looked at the indicted just formerly, and his outrage was naked in his eyes. also he turned to the Prosecutor. He was then to see justice for his dead son, and he'd not let himself down by losing his countenance.

The Prosecutor asked his name and circumstances. He answered easily in a low voice in which pride and anguish were inversely mixed.

The Prosecutor refocused to the indicted where she stood, body corpus, face prevented as though she set up it too delicate to meet his eyes. " And who's she? " he demanded.

"Anaya, " Stroban replied. " The widow of my son- in- law's family. She came in her time of need, and we took her in and treated her as our own. " His voice cracked. He plodded to control it. " And she repaid us with covetousness, rage and murder! "

There was a ripple of horror around the room, a admixture of hunger and fear.

The judge leaned forward, his face grave, the lines around his mouth deep and hard. "That's what we're then to test, and to prove, aye or nay."

"Of course, my lord, " Stroban conceded bleakly. " It's right that judgement should be seen. It's the law, and necessary to a just and cultivated life."

The judge jounced. " Justice will be served, I promise you, and great and everlasting justice, deeper than men will fluently grasp."

The Prosecutor permitted himself to smile. The Judge was a proud man, indeed a little arrogant, and he'd constantly intrude where it wasn't demanded, because he liked the sound of his own voice. But he'd rule rightly. The Prosecutor would one day be a judge like him, with his strengths, but not his sins, not his pomposity or his conceit. Curious how snappily one could see that.

"You took her in and gave her a home? " he said audibly, just to confirm it for the court.

"Yes, " Stroban agreed. " It was no lower than our duty. "

The Prosecutor squinched. That sounded a little cold and tone-righteous. It wasn't the image he'd wished to display of the bereft family. " How long agone was this? " he said hastily.

"Just under a time."

"And how did she bear?" He must move them on to suppose about the indicted. He glanced at her, and saw no guilt in her face, no respect, only what sounded to be fear.

"At first, with modesty and gratefulness," Stroban answered. " All gentleness, modesty and obedience. " His face reflected the hurt of her treason.

The Prosecutor felt an inviting wrathfulness rise in him. Of all crimes necromancy rankled him the most, it was the capstone of everything wrong that deceived and destroyed. It denied honour, and humanity. He looked at the Judge and saw a suchlike wrathfulness in his high, thin face, the nausea and aversion that he felt himself, and the knowledge that he'd it within his power, at least this time, to discipline it as it should be penalized with death. Witches might have black trades, but they were still mortal, and once they were exposed, they could feel pain like anyone differently.

He controlled his face and his voice with difficulty, and only because he was certain of the outgrowth. Stroban was less certain. All his life he'd known right from wrong. Any man did, if he were honest in heart. And could there be any virtue lesser than to know verity and judge correctly? It was the foundation of all virtue. Too frequently evil prevailed. Had it not done so in his own house his beautiful son would not now be lying dead. Bertil, whom he'd raised so precisely, tutored every detail of honour and righteousness. And also this woman, with her cleverness, her unhappy horselaugh, her wild studies, had come into their home, taken in by charity, and first betrayed them by trying to betray Bertil down from his woman, and also when he'd rejected her she had hovered to kill him. And when he'd still refused, she had cast her spell, an act of deliberate murder.

The execution was speaking again. "How long did she bear this way, pretending love and obedience?"

"She noway stopped, " Stroban said with nausea for her dishonesty.

The Prosecutor looked at the Judge's face. Stroban hadn't been duped because of his own innocence and charity, his incapability to imagine similar duplicity. The man was tone-righteous, too quick to judge and condemn. It was a cold fault, an unattractive bone.

But the Judge would be shown the verity, and also it would be the time to act. There must be law. Rules must be made and kept, by everyone. Without rules there was chaos, and that was truly intimidating, the gateway to all darkness. Indeed the Judge must observe the law.

The Prosecutor wanted further details. " Did she work hard around the ranch? And the house? Was she veracious, as far as you know? Did she admire you, and your woman? Did she treat you with a courtesy and gratefulness that she owed you? "

"Oh yes," Stroban replied. " She was veritably careful. " He knew he must speak the exact verity, whatever it was. He'd committed no wrong, so it couldn't harm him, or his family.

The Prosecutor's eyes widened. " Your choice of words suggests that you suppose she planned commodity evil from the morning. Is that so? "

Stroban dithered for a moment. He believed that she had, but it was only in the hindsight of what she had done. He hadn't known it also. He looked at her standing in her chains, and wondered how he could have been so eyeless. It was his own innocence that had dazed him.

"No," he admitted audibly. "I shouldn't have inferred that. I don't know what was in her mind. But she was attracted to poor Bertil from the launch, that was plain. At the time I believed it was only recognition of his virtuousness. Everyone liked Bertil. " Emotion crushed him and he was unfit to recapture control of himself for several twinkles. He saw pity in the Judge's eyes, and admiration, but neither would have anything to do with his opinions.

"Please continue, " the Prosecutor urged. " How did the indicted show this affection, precisely? "

Stroban forced himself to undergird his voice. " She helped him around the ranch. "

"How? "

"She was clever. " He said the word so it was half a curse. " She had ideas for perfecting effects. And she was clever with numbers, and measures. " He said the last plaintively. It was measures she had used to kill Bertil, although he still didn't know how.

"She bettered your yield? " the Judge intruded, leaning forward over the ancient bench, his sleeve hiding some of the poems on it. " She made life easier for you, better? "

Stroban felt a swell of wrathfulness. He was making her sound good! " For a while, " he admitted. " Oh, she was clever! "

The Prosecutor was irked. It showed in his expression, and the nervous clenching and unclenching of his fists. This was his home and the Judge was trespassing. " Were you thankful for this help " he cut across. " Did you wish it? "

"At the time, of course we were," Stroban said.

"All of you? Your woman, Enella, and your son- in- law, Korah, as well? "

"Of course."

"You all trusted the indicted? " He refocused to where she stood, her face white, her eyes concave and frighted indeed though her head was still high. Did she realize yet that there was no escape for her?

"Yes, " Stroban answered. " Why should we not? "

"Indeed. Tell us what happed to change your mind? "

Stroban felt his stomach wringing with the pain of memory, and yet he was on the point of chancing justice. It was over to him, his word, his saying what was right and true. He must be exact.

"There was a quarrel between Korah and Anaya, the indicted. " He avoided looking at her now. "I did n't know what it was about at the time... "

"Korah will tell us, " the Prosecutor assured him. " Please go on. "

Stroban adhered . " A many days latterly there was a more serious quarrel. That same evening Anaya said that if Bertil didn't do as she had told him to, also the barn roof would delve in and kill him. " He could slightly say the words. The scene was sculpted indelibly in his mind, Anaya standing in the kitchen, her hair crack in a copperred strip, the sun warming her face, the smells of cooking around them, the door open to the yard beyond and the lowing of the cattle in the distance. It was another world from this. They couldn't also have imagined the horror that awaited them.

The court was silent, faces still with fear.

"And how did Bertil reply to her? " the Prosecutor asked.

"He said she was wrong, " Stroban rumored. " My poor son! He'd no idea. " His voice caught in a sob. " He did n't believe in necromancy. "

There was a shiver around the room. People shifted in their seats, near to loved bones.

"But you do? " the Prosecutor claimed.

Stroban was angry, and hysterical . He looked at the Judge and saw wrathfulness in him too, at the asininity of the question, maybe? Also he saw commodity differently in the high-gutted, curious face, passionate one moment, ascetic the coming. It was a long, breathless moment before he understood that it also was fear. He had tasted the power of witchery, and he knew there was nothing to cover ordinary men except righteousness, and the exact observance of the law.

But if the Judge knew that, really knew it, also there was stopgap for them. He squared his shoulders and lifted his chin. "Of course I do! But I know that just men, biddable men, can master it! "

There was a murmur of admiration around the room, like a swell of the drift. Faces turned to the indicted, tight with abomination and fear.

"Had you ever allowed before that the barn roof would collapse?" the Prosecutor asked.

"Of course not! " Stroban was angry. "It rests on a great post, thick as a tree box!"

"Was anyone in the barn when this happed, piecemeal from your son?"

"No, just Bertil, and one of the oxen."

"I see. Thank you. The protector may wish to ask you commodity. "

Stroban turned to face the youthful man who now rose to his bases. He was a complete discrepancy to the Prosecutor. Far from being arrogant, he looked full of mistrustfulness, indeed confused, as if he'd no idea what he was going to say or do.

And indeed he didn't have. The whole proceeding was out of his control. When he'd spoken with Anaya before he'd believed her when she had said she was innocent. Now he didn't know what to suppose, nor did he have any faith in himself to achieve a just trial for her. Maybe the Judge would help him? But when he looked at the Judge, his long, pale face sounded as hugely confused as he was himself.

The protector turned to Stroban, cleared his throat and began. " We're deeply sorry for your grief. " He dithered. He must say commodity to the point, but what? " Where was the indicted when this tragedy happed? "

Stroban's face was a mask of wrathfulness, his voice grandly- pitched. " You say ' tragedy' as if it were a natural happening! It was necromancy! She made the roof fall in, exactly as she told him she would, if he didn't submit to her lust. But he was a righteous man, and he refused, so she killed him! "

There was a shiver of horror around the room. People reached for phylacteries.

The protector turned to the Judge for help, but the Judge did nothing. He sounded just as lost and overwhelmed. The protector turned back to Stroban. "I asked you where was she?"

"I do n't know, " Stroban said sullenly. " Out in the fields nearly, she told us. "

"Not in the barn?"

"Of course not! She did n't need to be there to make it be. Do n't you know anything about witchery? "

"No, I do n't. Maybe you would be good enough to instruct me? "

Stroban's cheeks flamed. "I know nothing moreover! What do you suppose I am? But it's important and wicked, and all good people who love verity and the law must fight against it with every strength they have. We must see that justice is done. It's our only protection. "

There were nods of agreement, a admixture of fear and an attempt at assurance.

The Defender knew he'd negotiate nothing with Stroban. It would be better to stay for his woman.

But when the Prosecutor called Enella she echoed exactly what her hubby had said, nearly in the same words. The Prosecutor sat down again, wholly satisfied.

The Defender rose. " You agreed that the indicted was veritably fond of your son, " he began, not relatively sure where he intended the question to lead. He glanced at Anaya, and saw a strange kind of peace in her eyes. He turned back to Enella. " In what ways did she show this? "

Enella was confused. " Why... the usual ways, I suppose. "

"And what are they? " he pressed.

"She... she talked with him fluently, comfortably. She made him laugh, without telling the rest of us what it was about. "

"You felt barred?"

"No! Of course not! " Now she was confused as well. She had been tricked into saying commodity she hadn't meant to.

"Why not?" he asked. "It sounds as if you were barred."

She looked at Stroban, also down again. “It was exactly as my hubby said, she wanted him for herself, in malignancy of the fact that he was married to her dead hubby’s family, whom she should have loved and fete . It was because of Korah that Bertil took Anaya in in the first place. Only a wicked woman would be so ungrateful! ” Enella was hysterical of query. She liked order. It was the only way to be safe.

“It sounds from what you say as if Bertil also liked her, ” the protector refocused out. “ Are you certain that she wasn't simply responding to him? After all, he was her host, so to speak. The head of her ménage. ”

Enella was hysterical . Stroban wasn't helping her. She looked at the Judge.

The Judge leaned forward over the bench, his face tense and unhappy. He goggled at the protector. “ I can not see where you're leading. Stay on the given path, if you please. ”

Enella relaxed again. The Judge was a decent man, a fair man. There was no need to be hysterical after all.

“I ’m sorry, my lord, ” the protector apologized. He was confused again. He looked at Anaya where she stood impeccably still. Her face was white, as if exhausted by plunging from stopgap to despond, and back again. Her shoulders drooped, as if the courage of a many moments ago had slipped from her. He'd promised her that he'd do his stylish, and so far he'd been pathetic. He must do better.

He took a step towards her, signaling his hand. “ We've heard that Anaya, ” he used her name tone- purposely, “ liked to make Bertil laugh. She helped him in his work, because she was clever, and inventive. Is that true? ” He knew that Enella would agree that it was, her hubby had formerly said so, and she'd noway contradict him.

“Yes, ” she said lugubriously.

“She made new suggestions for effectiveness and skill, effects that hadn't been done before? ” he pressed, beginning to see a bitsy light of stopgap.

There was only one possible answer, to have denied it would have been ridiculous. “ Yes.”

“So she was cleverer than Korah, or than any of you? ”

“Well... ”

“Or you would have allowed of them for yourselves, before she came? ”

“Well... yes, I suppose so. ”

The protector was beginning to feel more. He looked at the Judge and saw a spark of stopgap in his eyes also, a slight straightening of his shoulders and easing of the muscles of his jaw. It gave him courage to go on. He felt less alone. “ Surely it must be true? ”

Enella said nothing.

The protector was sorry for her, but he couldn't let her deny it.

The Judge looked at her, his face gentle. “ You must answer, ” he told her.

“Yes, ” she said veritably still, her face filled with unhappiness.

“Thank you, ” the Defender conceded. “ So Korah had to have seen it also? ”

“I do n’t know! ” It was a taradiddle , and the scarlet guilt swamped up her face. She must have felt its heat. “ I imagine she did. ”

“Maybe she was angry? Could that be what the quarrel was about? ”

“I do n’t know! ” That was the nonfictional verity, the letter of the law if not the spirit. She hid in the safety of that, looking to the Judge for protection, and from the easing of the severity of her body, believing she entered it.

The protector thanked her and gave her leave to go.

The Prosecutor called Korah, handsome, angry, thin- lipped. She walked into the Square knowing exactly what she was going to say. It had been sitting in her heart like a black weight since the first time she had seen Bertil laughing with Anaya and realized that while fidelity would hold him to Korah, but, if not now, also soon, it would be Anaya he loved, Anaya who touched the man within and awoke his heart and his dreams. In that day her abomination was born.

The Prosecutor faced her, arrogant and angry. She faced him exactly meeting his eyes. He'd not treat her as he'd dastardly, biddable Enella. Korah wasn't funny or imaginative, or beautiful, but she understood people. She could see right through the façade, the pretences, to the weakness within. And the Judge would help. She had been watching him, the high, thin face, the tight mouth. He was just like her. He understood what it was like to be mocked, to be left out, indeed in your own home. He could see the need for justice now. It wasn't vengeance, it was what Anaya merited, not for necromancy, there was no similar thing, but for theft.

"Anaya is your family's widow, and after his death you took her in and gave her a home? " The Prosecutor was repeating the important data, just to remind the crowd, and the Judge.

"Yes, I did, " Korah answered. noway say further than you need to, that was the way to make miscalculations.

"And she repaid you by helping in the house and on the ranch?"

"Yes. She was veritably professed at it. " Be generous. It sounded better than grudging praise. And it was the verity.

"Better than you?"

"In some ways, not in others. " Do n't let them see the covetousness. Do n't look at Anaya in case your studies are there in your face, in malignancy of all you can do. She looked rather at the Judge. He understood, it was egregious in his expression, the eyes, the lips. maybe he too had been betrayed? It must have been long agone. He was dried up now, withered, withered outside.

The Prosecutor was talking again. " Was your hubby a handsome man, fascinating? "

"Yes. " Oh yes, that was true. " Everyone liked him. It was far further than aesthetics . It was his manner, his honesty, his warmth, his horselaugh, his kindness. " All that was so sorrowfully true. It hurt to say it now for all these prurient, superstitious people gaping at her. Damn Anaya! They should burn her! Let her feel the fire on her body, consume her meat and destroy it, indeed if they couldn't make it burn her soul on the inside.

"So you weren't surprised when your family- in- law was attracted to him?"

In malignancy of herself Korah's eyes were drawn to Anaya and for an moment they looked at each other. Korah saw faith floundering with fear of pain, of failure, of maximum loneliness, and palm was like honey on her lingo.

"No, " she answered. " I believed she'd recognize her place as my family and my guest. I had no idea she had... powers. "

The Prosecutor had seen the exchange. " Bertil rejected her? " he asked.

"Yes. He was veritably worried by it. He set up it grossly dishonorable. He was revolted. "

"What did Anaya do? "

Korah smiled veritably slightly, just a bitsy movement of the lips. " She said that if he didn't change his mind and come to her, also the barn roof would delve in and crush him to death. " No bone could catch her out in that. They weren't the exact words, but the meaning was the same. Timour had heard her say it, and he could swear. He was so transparently honest everyone would believe him.

"And did he change his mind? "

There was a silence in the room as if no bone breathed. The sun outside sounded a world down.

"Of course not, " Korah said. " I do n't suppose he was hysterical , but indeed if he'd been, he'd rather have failed than give in to such a thing. "

A hundred voices in the room muttered blessing, and sympathy.

Anaya stood with her eyes closed, as if demanding to summon all her strength just to remain upright.

"It seems we've lost an exceptionally fine man with his death, " the Prosecutor said with relish. " maybe evil always seeks to destroy that which is purest and stylish. "

The Judge sounded about to say commodity. He drew in his breath, also let it out again in a shriek, as if some inner resolution had prevailed.

"Eventually, doxy, " the Prosecutor said, " How long had that barn stood with that roof safe and secure? "

"Seventy times."

"Thank you. " He looked trim, completely satisfied with himself.

The Defender took his place. He sounded indeed more confused than ahead.

"I've nothing to ask you. "

She stood down, glancing at the Judge's pinched, unhappy face, and for an instant seeing her own future in it, old and alone, eaten by bitterness and tone- nausea. also she drove it from her mind and returned to her seat beside Enella, but a dispassionateness remained in the hole of her stomach.

The Prosecutor called Timour, who verified all that Korah had said. He looked trustingly at the protector as he approached. He felt sorry for all of them, especially Anaya. He'd liked her, as he knew Bertil had. She had sounded funny and kind and stalwart. He'd had no idea that she had any detriment in her, still lower that she had knowledge of the black trades. He still set up it hard to believe. But he did know barns, and he knew oxen. He said as important when the Defender asked him.

"Oh yes. It's my trade, " he agreed.

"Did you see this barn after it had fallen in? "

"Yes. I wanted to know what had happed. It's important, in case it should be again. " He looked at the Judge to see if he understood. He sounded to. He'd the air of a stalwart man, not only a strength in his face but a gentleness as well, as if he anticipated the stylish in people. He was the kind of man Timour liked, wise without arrogance, kind without sentiment. " I saw it ahead, you see, " he explained. " They had been keeping oxen in it for a long time, my lord. Big beasts, and veritably heavy, veritably important. They like to lean against the posts and rub their tails, scratch them, as it were. However, sooner or latterly they 'll dislodge the pole from its base, If you do n't keep an eye on them. I advised Bertil about it. He was a good man, and my friend, but he did put effects off. " He glanced at Stroban an reason. " I 'm sorry, but that's true. Anaya saw it, and she advised him too. But he was always going to do it hereafter. I suppose when hereafter eventually came, it was too late. "

There was silence for a moment, a consummation, a wakening from a dream both good and bad. It was the Judge who asked the question, not the protector. " Could the ox have pushed against it while Bertil was there, and knocked it over when it was at the most vulnerable? "

"I suppose it must have done, " Timour answered. " It ran out just as the roof buckled and caved in. It got bruised by some of the falling timbers. He should have put it out before he began to work, but he ca n't have. "

"Necromancy! " Stroban cried out, rising to his bases, his face flushed. "It's still her fault! "

"No! " the Defender said with unforeseen strength, reeling round, his mask flying, his arm outstretched. " A man delayed mending his barn until the post was seriously weakened. It's a tragedy. It isn't a crime. " He looked to the Judge, raising his eyes to the high seat, the dark poems carried in the wood. " My lord, I ask that you gasp Anaya innocent of this poor man's death, free these people of the fear of witchery, and allow them to suffer for their loss without fear or blame. She didn't hang him, she advised him. And tragically, he didn'tlisten.However, we shouldn't be then moment mourning him, seeing necromancy where there's only covetousness, If he'd done. "

Stroban looked desperately at the Judge, and saw a man filtered by the details of the law and unfit to see the lesser spirit of it, a man who understood loss but not love. He was a small man, who could in the end come a concave man.

Enella looked at the Judge and saw a man who kept to the safe path, always, wherever it led, overhead or down, and there was an emptiness in it that nothing would fill.

Korah saw what she had honored before, only this time it wasn't for an moment. It would always be there, whether she looked at it or not.

The Prosecutor was angry. He saw a Judge whose arrogance had allowed him to lose control of the court. He didn't know how it had happed, or why palm had inexplicably come defeat.

Timour and the Defender both saw an upsurge of sanguinity. Hope had come out of nowhere, and subdued the error and despair.

The Judge pronounced Anaya innocent. The court was dismissed and people poured out into the dark, gulping the sweet air, leaving the room empty except for Anaya and the Judge.

He moved his right hand veritably slightly, just two fritters from the face of the bench. The chains fell down. She stood free, rubbing her wrists and stretching her paining shoulders.

"You did well, " he said still. He was smiling.

"I misdoubted, " she answered. It was a concession.

"Of course you did, " he agreed, and as he spoke his face changed, it came wiser, stronger, passion and horselaugh burned in it, and an inexpressible gentleness. However, it would be worth little, " If it were easy. You haven't yet perfected faith. Don't anticipate so much of yourself. For assignments learned hastily or without pain are empty. "

"Will they understand? " she asked.

"That they were the bones on trial, and that the judgement was your own? Oh yes. In time. Whether they will pay the cost of change is another thing. But there's love, and there's stopgap. We are far from the end. " His cloak lustered and began to dissolve. She could no longer see his shoulders, only his strong, slender hands and his face. "Now I've another charge for you. "

She looked at him, at the white fire around him. All she could distinguish was his smile, and his voice, and a great peace shone within her. "Yes?"

Chapter No. 6: She's Not There

Nothing is vulnerable to Glamour.

In the ten times she'd had the gift, Darla had noway come across anybody who had seen through it, far as she could tell. Old, youthful, men, women, — it wisecracked everybody, every time.

Not that she 'd need it then Fifteen bases down, the widow Bellingham inspired completely- dressed upon her bed. The old lady had put down a bottle of veritably precious champagne before at the party, and Darla could presumably could bang a Chinese gong and not rouse her, but still...

She opened the last hole of the jewel box, her movements slow and careful. The smell of cedar drifted up from the intricately- sculpted rustic box, which was presumably worth further than Darla's auto.

Ah. Then we go...

It was an round leg about the size of a tableware bone. Inset into the platinum were thirty- some diamonds, fancy yellows, the maturity of them a carat or so each. Not worth as much as clears and nowhere near the value of the violent pinks or fancy blues riming the pieces in the top hole, of course, but that was the point. These were good monuments — good but not outstanding, and with what she could get from her hedge, plenitude to keep her going for six months.

One- carat gems of this grade were easy to move.

She limited herself to a job every three or four months, enough to keep her below heavy police radar — or at least it had done so for eight times.

Truth was, it had been nearly too easy. noway a really close call. At first, it it had sounded a grand adventure, but it was not long before it turned into just a part- time job, no more instigative than shopping for fruit at New Seasons Market. Go by, pick out the organic apples you like, leave — without paying and take a many months out, ta dah!

Disappointing in a way how easy it was, though clearly better than working for a living...

Six or seven million in fine jewelry then, and that just the dailywear stuff. The really good pieces would be in a bank vault nearly...

Darla wrapped the leg in a forecourt of black velvet and slipped it into her jeans fund. She slid the jewelry box's hole closed.

As always, she was tempted to clean the box out, but she knew better. Unique pieces were hard to move, worth only what the loose monuments would bring, unless you wanted to mess around trying to find a crooked collector, and that was parlous. This particular leg? It might not be missed for weeks or months. The top- hole stuff sure; the nethermost hole? perhaps the widow would noway indeed notice. When you could go by and flump down a million bucks for a brooch or a choker without having to look at your checkbook balance? A leg worth a couple hundred grand? Shoot, that was virtually costume jewelry...

So, she 'd take just the one piece.

The perfect crime, after all, wasn't one where the bobbies could n't figure out who did it; it was one the bobbies noway indeed heard about...

Darla uttered the cantrip just before she pushed open the stair door into the apartment structure's lobby. When she stepped through, she looked the same to herself, save for a slight bluish gleam to her skin that told her the Glamour was lit.

The guard at the office looked up. "Morning, Mr. Millar. Beforehand start moment, hey? "

Darla beamed and sketched a two- cutlet salutation at the guard.

The fortified man touched a button on his press and the structure's door slid open. As she left, Darla switched one hand over her shoulder, in what she allowed was a friendly gesture. Quietly, of course. Her Glamour wisecracked the eyes, but not the cognizance if she spoke, she'd sound like a twenty- commodity woman and not the sixty- commodity man she picked as a disguise.

She had been careful coming down the stairs to avoid the surveillance cams, too, since her trick would n't wisecrack them, moreover.

When the realMr. Millar exited for his morning walk, the guard would n't say anything — he would n't want anybody to suppose he was crazy...

It was a fantastic thing, her trick; indeed, if it had a couple downsides She had to touch notoriety before it would work on them, and do that within a day, since the goods of the touch faded down after that. Still, it was emotional.

She had no idea why or how she had come by it. She had been set up in a dumpster as a baby, raised in an orphanage. The words to the cantrip were from a dream she 'd had on the night she turned sixteen. Ultimately, she had come to realize that, ever, the dream had come true.

Magic? No similar thing, everybody knew that. But then she was. She 'd wondered about it over the times. She 'd cautiously nosed around in a many places, but noway set up any other real magic, only people faking it. Why did it work? How? She did n't know. Still, you did n't have to be a druggist to strike a match, and supposedly you did n't need to know jack about magic to use the stuff. Case in point.

Fussing over the reasons might drive her nuts if she let it, so she did n't try any further. She just thanked whatever gods there might be for bestowing it upon her and that was that.

She had a auto, but she infrequently used it on a job where public transportation was available. She walk to the machine stop. The TriMet motorist would see her as a white-haired Japanese man, since she had touched his shoulder before in the day when she 'd ridden the machine in this direction. She'd exit six blocks from her apartment and walk home. nothing could connect Darla Wright to the precious Portland extension enthralled by the widow Bellingham, indeed if the woman ever did notice she 'd been burgled.

Smooth as oil painting on glass, no muss, no fuss, just like always, and she planned to sleep in until at least noon.

Life was good.

Darla rambled into her neighborhood Starbucks, coming to Fred Meyer's, and gobbled the spices of brewed coffee and lately ignited after's. She was gibing for a fattening cherry development she figured she 'd earned, when she banged into a good- looking joe about thirty who stopped suddenly ahead of her in the line.

"Oh, sorry, " he said, turning to steady her. " My fault. " He smiled. Nice teeth. Black hair, blue eyes, rugged features, enough well- erected under a dark green T- shirt and snug jeans. Three or four times aged than she was, but that was nothing.

"No problem, " she said. She returned the smile.

Ice cream, she allowed, looking at him. To go with the confection, hey...?

No... She could n't. Not moment. She had to meet Harry at two, and she 'd slept past noon, so Ice Cream then would have to stay. Business before pleasure.

There were plenitude of other men in the pond, and she was going to have free time to do a little fishing, lots of time...

Nothing as egregious as running a pawn shop, Harry had a guitar store, a hole- in- the-wall place twenty twinkles from Portland, in Beaverton. Beaverton was where Portlanders went to buy fast food and shop at the 7- Elevens, a bedroom community that had formerly been wetlands and filbert vineyards and beaver- dammed aqueducts.

The guitars at Harry's ran from a many hundred bucks up to ten or fifteen thousand on the high end, substantially aural and classicals, and the place actually did a enough good business. Moment being Sunday, the shop was closed, but Harry answered the bell at the aft door. She awaited while the four big and heavy cinches snicked and clicked, bolts sliding back, and the door, made of thick sword plate, swung still open on waxed hinges. Trust a crook to know how to cover his own stuff.

The shop smelled of wood, and some kind of finish that wasn't unwelcome, a sharp, turpentine- y scent.

"Layla. How nice to see you, as always."

Indeed Harry did n't get her real name. Darla was veritably careful.

"Harry. How business? "

"I ca n't complain. Come in. Some tea? " He was seventy- five, bald, thin, and wore thick spectacles that kept slipping down his nose. He allowed she was hot, though he 'd noway made a move on her.

"Thanks."

She sat at a table while Harry made tea. " Oolong moment, " he said.

Ultimately, he sat the storming mug in front of her.

"So, youngster, whaddya got for me? "

She produced the leg, opened the velvet wrapping.

"Ah. " He picked it up, pulled a loupe from his shirt fund, held the leg up to the light.

"Quality monuments. Nice cuts, nothing outstanding. Say... fifty? "

"What, did I get stupid since you saw me last? Eighty, " she said.

He smiled. " Might could go sixty, because I like you. "

"It's a steal at eighty, Harry. Two and a quarter for the bigger monuments, and perhaps another ten or fifteen for the little bones. Plus seven, eight hundred for the platinum. Pushing a quarter million, and you can pocket half that. "

"Honey, we both know it's a steal at any price, but since I 'll have to fly down to Miami to move the jewels, sixty is a gift. You know how I detest air trip "

"Miami? What's wrong with Seattle? "

He pulled the loupe off and put the piece onto the table. " Too warm for Seattle. Indeed broken up, thirty monuments this close will have to be moved a many at a time. Could take me months. Who has that kind of time at my age? "

"Warm? The, uh, former proprietor does n't indeed know it's gone. "

"Alas, dear girl, I 'm hysterical she does. Mrs. Bellingham, widow of the late Leo Bellingham, proprietor of sword manufactories and ockyards, right? presumably pays her boy toys further than this curio is worth, but she has surely missed it."

Darla shook her head. "How could that be? And how do you know it?"

He signed. " perhaps moment was force day. Or it was a gift from a special friend with novelettish value. Who can say? All I know is, I talked to Benny the Nod this morning and he said the Portland bobbies had come to call upon him beforehand, signaling a picture of this veritably item. " He tapped the leg.

"Sweet Jesus, " she said.

"I misdoubt He'd have any part of this, sweet, though you can tithe if you want. So, sixty?"

"Yeah, well, I guess. Sure. "

They drank more tea and he babbled on about some new classical guitar he 'd just bought, Osage Orange this, cedar that, Sloane tuners, a genuine Carrith, look at the little owl inlay then it all flowed into one observance and out the other. How unlucky was this? That the old woman had discovered the theft within hours of it passing? That bring her at least twenty thousand bones!

There was just no justice...

As Darla drove her British racing-green Cooper Mini convertible along television trace back toward Portland, she relaxed a little. Yeah, okay, her rearmost theft had been discovered too snappily, but she was still sixty thousand bones richer, Harry's cash, in used hundreds, was put away away in her bag right there on the passenger seat. Life was still good. The sun was shining, the top was down, it was a lovely June autumn, and she was free to spend the coming many months droning about, doing whatever she damned well pleased. Better than a poke in the eye with a sharp stick, hey?

She stopped at the light next to the Chrysler dealership on Canyon Road, tapping her fritters on the steering wheel as the Beatles sang " Hey, Jude " on the oldies station.

A stocky teenage boy in baggy films and a sweatshirt with arrestment sleeves, a brim-backward baseball cap pulled downward , his bases shod in big, clonky, unattractive basketball shoes, strutted across the road in front of her. She could n't see his eyes behind the dark tones he wore. Oh, please, sprat! Who do you suppose you 're fooling?

When he was nearly once, on the passenger side, he refocused behind her and said, " Holy shit! Look at that! "

Darla turned to see what had impressed this wanna- be gansta sprat.

She caught a blur in her supplemental vision, and turned back just in time to see the sprat hitch her bag —

"Fuck —!"

Darla put the auto into neutral, set the boscage , and jumped out of the auto. She chased the sprat, but he'd a head start and he was a lot faster than he looked. He put on a burst of speed and she lost him behind the auto dealership.

And what she have done if she 'd caught him? protest his burro? She did n't know anything about martial trades. She had a nice folding cutter, but unfortunately, that had been in her bag, too.

Son- of-a-bitch!

By the time she got back to her auto, there was a line of business piled up behind it. She stalked back to the auto, gave the cutlet to the fool behind her laying on his cornucopia.

Fuck, fuck, fuck, fuck!

Sixty thousand bones!

The hell of it was, she could n't do anything about it! She could hear the discussion with the bobby in her head Ah, you say you had sixty thousand bones in cash in your bag? What's it you do for a living again, Miss?

Shit!

So much for the idea of six or eight months of goofing off. She was going to have to find another score. Soon She was enough important tapped out. She 'd been counting on last night's job.

No fucking justice...

Darla flashed back a line she'd heard nearly, when some journalist was canvassing a notorious purloiner. "So, Willie, why do you burglarize banks? " And his answer had been " Because that's where the plutocrat is... "

Presumably noway said that, but it made the point you want to see who has the bling, you have to go where they flash it.

Which was why she was at a posh event for some notorious author at the Benton Hotel in Portland. Once she was past the gate keeper, having him see her as notoriety who showed up at these effects that he knew by sight, she came herself again, but she had to look the part, so she had dressed up for it. Heels, a black slinky dress, a simple beachfront of good black plums, her short, dark hair nicely nominated. nothing inside would bother her, though the crowd was thick enough that notoriety gentled her on the burro as she squeezed through on her way to the bar. supposedly that cherry confection had n't added enough weight to matter...

She got a club soda pop with lime, also started shopping...

She winnowed her choices to two possible.

One was a forty- commodity woman with gorgeous red hair and a great figure she worked hard to keep looking that way. She had had a little plastic work done on her face, veritably subtle, but neutralize by a bot oxed forepart that might as well have been sculpted from marble. She wore emeralds earrings, a choker, a ring that had to run four carats, all matching settings in unheroic gold. The dress was a delicate yellow that went with the jewelry. Quarter million in tones of green fire. Nice.

The other prospect was a joe, perhaps thirty- five, in an Armani tux. He was scourged and fit, with a little argentine in his hair, and an easy smile, and though he was n't sporting any monster jewels, he did wear a Patek Philippe watch — she guessed it was a Goliath Nautilus in rose gold, worth about thirty grand wholesale. He'd one ring on his right hand, a gold nugget inset with a black opal the size of a song, that flashed Chinese jotting in multiple colors as the opal caught the light when he raised his champagne glass to belt . That good an Australian opal might go ten grand. She would n't want either the watch or the ring, they 'd be too hard to move, but he 'd presumably have other pieces laying around...

Men were both harder and lightly for her. Looking like she did, she could get close to them and touch them enough to get passions for notoriety she could come. And further than a many rich men had offered to take her home for their own purposes, of course, but still, it got her a lot of intelligence for a after visit...

So, the emerald lady or the opal joe?

Indeed as she allowed this, the opal joe looked up and noticed her. He smiled at the man he was talking to, said commodity, and sauntered in her direction.

Well, look at this. If he was going to do the work? Perhaps that was a good sign....

"What's a nice girl like you doing at a stuffy event like this?"

"Staying for you, it seems, " she said. She gave him her high wattage smile.

He held his champagne glass over in a silent toast, as if to admit her response to his pick-up line. " I 'm Arlo St. Johns, " he said.

"Layla Harrison, " she said, giving him a name she 'd made up for herself in the orphanage times agone. One of housemothers who was n't too awful had been a big addict of the English gemstone irruption of the early sixties, and had advanced Darla her books about the subject. She had discovered that Eric Clapton had written the song " Layla " after having fallen for George Harrison's woman, Patti. That woman must have been commodity, Darla had decided, since she had been the alleviation for at least three notorious gemstone songs "commodity," by Harrison when he 'd been with the Beatles; " Layla; " and " awful Tonight, " by Clapton.

Ran in the family, too — Pattie's little family had been Donovan's poet for " Jennifer, Juniper, " and had gone on to marry Mick Fleetwood of Fleetwood Mac...

"Penny for your studies? " he said.

"Worth further than that, I suppose. "

"No doubt. Want to go get a drink or commodity nearly a little less crowded? "

"What did you have in mind? "

"My place is important quieter. "

She smiled. "Why not? Seen one pen, seen them all... "

Johns had a high- rise apartment town, and he drove them to it in a black Cadillac Escalade, still had the new auto smell. Sixty, seventy thousand bucks worth of auto. This was shaping up to be a delightful evening. Guy was good- looking, well- mannered, was obviously doing well enough to drive a high- end SUV and to sport precious, tasteful jewelery. Bound to have commodity laying around his place worth lifting.

She did n't have a lot of rules in her biz, but one of them was that she did n't get intimate — well, not too intimate with her marks. Not that this was ironclad — she had slipped a couple of times but it made her feel shamefaced robbery from notoriety she 'd slept with, and she did n't need that. Darla had erected a enough good vindication about stealing from the rich and their insurers who would n't miss it; if she went to bed with notoriety and had a really good time? It would feel wrong to take his stuff.

Pretending not to look, she fluently managed to see the figures he punched into the alarm keypad just inside the door. She committed them to memory, converting them to letters. The first letter of each word corresponded to the number of its position in the ABC therefore 78587 came GHEHG, which in turn came a crazy but memorable judgment Great Hairy mammoths detest Giraffes...

The apartment was gorgeous, decorated by notoriety with plutocrat and taste. oil painting oils, fancy handwrought paper lights, Oriental carpets some family in Afghanistan must have spent times making. upmarket cabinetwork, more comfortable than grabby.

While St. Johns erected them drinks at his wet bar, she went into the restroom, took her cell phone from her bag, and programmed it to ring in thirty twinkles. That would give them enough time to have a drink and talk a little, but not get to the rolling- around- and-breaking- precious- cabinetwork stage.

She went back into the living room.

St. Johns was funny, smart, and twenty twinkles into their discussion over perfect martinis, she was allowing perhaps she'd sleep with him rather of burgling him. That would be okay.

But, she reminded herself, she was beggared. She had a couple thousand in the bank, but her apartment rent was due, her auto note, and her fridge was substantially empty. She demanded the plutocrat further than she demanded to get laid.

A shame. He really was delightful. He was some kind of importer, specializing in Pacific Rim agedness, he said, and there were a many pieces of Polynesian or Hawaiian or other islet art precisely set out then and there that she suspected were presumably worth a small fortune. Jewelry she knew, oil and form, she did n't have a indication.

He smiled at her. " So, what do you do when you are n't attending boring social gatherings? "

"Not much, I 'm hysterical . When my parents failed, they left me a fair- sized insurance policy. I had the plutocrat invested, so it brings in enough to keep the wolf from the door. I take classes in this and that, work out, travel a bit. Nothing veritably instigative. "

He smiled bigger.

She smiled back. Oh, this was n't just ice cream, this was Häagen Dazs Special Limited Edition Black Walnut, you could get fat just opening the tinderbox. The temptation surged in her, a warm surge. She had enough to pay the rent and auto note, slightly, she could buy some red sap and rice and veggies, make it another week before she had to have some further plutocrat...

In her bag, her cell phone began playing Pachelbel's Canon in D.

Crap! What to do? Shut the phone off and stay?

Because she wanted to do just that so much, she decided it was n't a good idea. A matter of discipline. However, that could lead her down a dangerous pitch, If she slipped. Just because it had always been good did n't mean it could n't go bad.

Oh, well. She smiled, brought her phone, touched a control.

"Hey, what's up? " A beat. also, " Oh, no! That's terrible! Are you each right? "

St. Johns raised an eyebrow at her.

"No, no, I 'll come over. I 'll see you in a little while. "

She snapped the phone shut. " I 'm sorry. That was my gal Maria, " she said. " Her fiancé just ditched her and she's in a terrible state. I need to go see her. "

"I knew it was too good to be true. I 'll give you a lift. "

"No, I 'll catch a hack. She lives way out in Hillsboro, I would n't ask you to do that. "

"It's no trouble. I do n't have anything additional planned. "

"Really, I appreciate it, but no. Could you, uh, give me your number? I 'd like to see you again. "

"Oh, yes. " He produced a business card that had nothing on it but his name and a phone number. "Take care of your friend, " he said, smiling. " And do call me. I 'd love to see you again. "

"I'll look forward to seeing you, " she said. Unfortunately, you wo n't know who I'm when I do...

"Let me call a hack."

"Thanks, Arlo."

"My pleasure."

After he called, he walked her to the door, and rested his hand on her shoulder. There was a moment when she allowed he would kiss her — and she would n't have expostulated but it passed.

Another road not taken.

Too bad, but that is how life was. Occasionally, business had to come ahead pleasure.

Her hack arrived. The night was warm, and she slid into the hack and gave the motorist an address near a stop where she could catch a MAX train to a station near her place.

"Yes, Mrs.," the motorist said. He looked to be about fifty, and from his accentuation, she guessed he was Indian, or Pakistani.

It really was too bad about St. Johns.

The cabbie was chatty, going on about the warm rainfall and how the Bull Run Resevoir was low for this time of time. She responded politely, formerly allowing of how she was going to burgle St. Johns's apartment. However, it would be a snap — she 'd come St, If the Glamour had worked on voices. Johns, tell the security joe she 'd lost her key, and have him let her into the place. Take commodity the mark would n't miss, and adios.

Too bad St. Johns was n't a mute —

Ah! stay a alternate, hold on, she had commodity then...

"Supplicate amnesty, Miss " the cabbie said.

"Huh? " She looked at him.

"You made an interjection? Are you in torture? "

She smiled. " Oh, oh, no, sorry. I was just allowing of commodity. I 'm fine. "

The cabbie smiled and jounced.

Actually, she was better than fine. She had come up with a atrocious idea. Why had n't it passed to her times ago? It was so simple.

She paid the cabbie, gave him a nice tip — what the hell, she 'd be flush again in a couple days, right? She walked to the MAX station. A light rail train arrived, and she got on, along with several others. She exited at the stop near her house. An old lady dressed in khaki britches and a tie- color T- shirt and handling shoes got off the train and set off at a fast walk ahead of her. The woman had long, steely argentine hair and a lot of smile wrinkles and was obviously in enough good shape from the pace she set. You could do worse than to be notoriety like that when you got old, Darla decided. But not for a real long time...

Johns demanded to be out of the structure, so she had to risk using her auto. She situated near the exit to the garage beforehand, and awaited to seeSt. Johns ' bin leave.

At about nine in the morning, the Escalade pulled out.

Okay, sprat, then we go...

Darla approached the structure's road entrance. She put a hand on the gatekeeper's sleeve as she asked to see the security man on duty.

Inside, she was conducted to the security office. The man behind it looked up.

"Help you, Miss" He stood and moved to the counter.

"Yes, I saw a auto situated out front and there were two men in it who sounded to be watching the entrance, " she said. " presumably it's nothing, but I allowed

I should say commodity about it. "

"Two men? What kind of auto? They still there? "

She signed. " I 'm not good with buses . Like a van, perhaps an SUV? Dark, kind of old, muddy? But they left. "

"Uh huh. You get get the license number, ma'am? "

She shook her head. "Sorry."

"Ah. Well. hear, we appreciate it. We 'll, uh, keep an eye out for it. " presumably allowing was a twit she was. Two men in a auto, right...

She reached out and touched his arm. "Presumably it's nothing, " she said. " But these days, you ca n't be too careful. "

" Yes, ma'am. That's true. "

Darla stepped into a doorway in the coming structure and lit the Glamour. Show time...

"Morning, Mr. St. Johns, " the gatekeeper said. He opened the heavy glass door.

Darla smiled and jounced, knowing that her disguise was perfect.

She walked to the security office.

"Mr. St. Johns. How may I help you joe? "

She shook his head and touched her throat. In a raspy voice as low as she could manage, Darla said, " Laryngitis. " She coughed.

"Oh, sorry to hear that. "

"Forgot my key," she said. Her voice was a passable reproduction of a sick frog.

"No problem, joe." The guard opened a wide hole, scrutinized the contents, and produced a door crucial. "Then you go. Drop it off whenever. "

Darla smiled, jounced, and coughed as she took the key.

Perfect. She did n't have to sound likeSt. Johns, she had set it up that her — his — voice was gone. Veritably clever, if she said so herself.

People were coming and going, and the guard's attention veered down from her.

There were n't any cameras on the elevators, at least none she 'd seen the night ahead, but she dallied until a couple other people arrived to ride up. They would see her as Darla, and if there was a retired camera on the elevator, the guard would see three people in it. How important track would he be keeping?

So far, it ran like a Swiss watch.

She opened the door, stepped outside — it would n't do for notoriety to see her rather of St. Johns, though they might assume she was his special friend, since she had a key.

Inside, she shut the door and reached for the alarm pad, but realized that it was green. He had n't indeed bothered to set it.

She shook her head. Man did n't turn on his alarm? He merited to have his stuff stolen. Lordy.

In the bedroom, it took all of ten seconds to find the jewelry box — it was leather, trimmed in brass, and it sat atop a dresser made of what looked like ebony.

Darla opened the box.

My. There were gold coins, loose gems, substantially diamonds, but a couple of emeralds, a diamond- speckled plutocrat clip that held three thousand bones in hundreds. There was a barred 5K mound of hundreds next to that, but the band was broken and two were missing. There were a dozen platinum coins and ten platinum one ounce beams, and several sets of cuff links and tie legs, done in varied gems — rubies, emeralds, sapphires...

Snappily, Darla decided what she could remove without it being incontinently noticed. There were thirty- two gold coins, Eagles, and she took two of those. Nineteen loose monuments, fourteen of which were one or two- carat, round- cut blue-white diamonds. She took one of the two- carat monuments, and one of the single carats. She took two hundreds from the plutocrat clip, three from the barred mound. One of the platinum coins, one of the beams. She considered the tie- fashions and cuff links and decided they were too fluently missed.

Okay, a quick total Couple gold Eagles, presumably worth eight hundred each. The platinum Eagle was worth fourteen, fifteen hundred, presumably, the rod a little less, say twelve hundred, and that was plutocrat in her fund, since they did n't have to be fended. The diamonds were clean and clear, figure six, eight thousand on the lower one, and at least twenty- five or thirty on the bigger one. lower Harry's cut on those, so say they were worth twenty thousand to her aggregate, if she was lucky. With the cash, she 'd net about twenty five grand aggregate. UnlessSt. Johns did an force, he probably would n't notice anything was gone, and she 'd buy herself three or four months of taradiddle - about time. Not nearly as good as what she had gotten from the widow's place, but she had that laryngitis trick, and that would come in handy.

Formerly again, it was tempting to lade it all into her fund — there was enough then to keep her from having to score again for a couple, three times, perhaps longer. But, no... More to stick with what had kept her out of jail for all this time, rapacity was a killer. She soughed, and closed the jewelry box.

As she turned to leave, she noticed the corner of a box protruding out from under the bed. A bed with black silk wastes on it, she also noticed, and neatly made.

She stopped, fraudulent, and pulled the box from under the bed. It was long, wide, and fairly flat, as big as a large wallet, if shallower. She opened the box...

It was full of thousand bone bills, piled into rows, fifteen across and eight down, and the bills were loose and substantially used.

Holy shit!

She picked up one mound, her breath coming briskly, and counted it. also another mound. A third. The first had thirty, the alternate twenty- eight, the third, thirty- three. Non-sequentially numbered.

She did some fast calculation. A hundred and twenty heaps, say thirty bills in each mound on average.

Three million six hundred thousand bones.

Oh, man!

What was St. Johns doing with this important cash under his bed?

Darla goggled at the cash. However, he might not indeed notice! She could take a hundred thousand, two hundred thousand, If she took one or two bills from each mound. And indeed if he did that, she was enough sure this was n't plutocrat he wanted anybody to know about — it had the smell of commodity not relatively legal...

Of course, she could n't just walk into a bank and flump down a couple hundred-thousand- bone bills and anticipate that to fly without raising questions; but Harry knew people who could move big notes without fur an eye and he 'd take ten or fifteen percent, no further than that...

Two bills from each mound. Two hunded and forty thousand bones, she could give Harry the two- carat blue-white for his cut and — no, she decided, she 'd put all that back. No point in risking this important for petty cash. With two hundred grand in her fund, she could take a long damn time before she had to make another score.

Yes. That is how she'd do it. Put the coins and gems back, pack a quarter of a million into her pockets — no more carrying it in pocketbooks, thank you veritably much — and walk down with a big smile under her Glamour...

Darla drove toward her place, using a long and winding route, to make sure she was n't followed. She was nearly home when she heard the sound of a police temptress. She looked into the rearview glass and saw a plain, tan Crown- Victoria with a blue light flashing on the dashboard behind her.

"Oh, shit! " she said. An icy surge washed over her, as if she 'd been drenched in liquid nitrogen, turning her stiff with fear.

She pulled to the check. This was n't a business stop.

An altitudinous, stocky, balding man alighted from the auto. He wore a cheap, poorly wrinkled suit and brown shoes, and a tie that failed to reach his belt. Might as well have had a neon sign over his head flashing out the word " Bobby! "

He walked to her motorist's door.

"Would you step out of the auto, please? "

"What's the trouble? Was I speeding? "

"No, lady, I 'm a operative, I do n't do business tickets. Out then, please, and keep your hands where I can see them. "

Dead. She was dead. She had considered it over the times, what she'd do if she was ever caught, but it had noway sounded real to her, it had been so theoretical.

What was she going to do?

The Glamour.

Of course! In her panicked fear, she had forgotten she had a perfect armament. She 'd touch him, and when the moment was right, she 'd distract him, change, and that would be that!

The woman? she 'd say, when he turned around and saw an old man there, She went that way, she was running!

Okay, she 'd be okay, she could do this. He 'd have to stroke her down, and that would be enough, his hands on her would be fine. A touch was a touch.

"Over on the sidewalk, please, " he said.

She adhered.

"What did I do? " she asked.

"You do n't need me to tell you that. Step in there, please. "

He refocused to a gate that lead to what looked like a small theater.

"Excuse me? "

"We do n't want to do this out then. "

"Do what out then?! "

The fear she 'd felt came back. What was going on?

"Open the gate, please. "

She did. He shut the wrought iron behind them. " Wow, look at that, " he said.

She turned. " Wh- what? "

When she turned back to look at the bobby he was gone.

In his place was an old woman.

Darla lowered. She knew this woman from somewere... ah, it was the old lady on the MAX train...

"Or this? " the old woman said, in a substantially mannish voice.

The woman lustered , and of a moment, Darla set up herself looking at the hack motorist who had taken her home fromSt. Johns —

And also, like a strobe light blinking on and off, the hack motorist came the teenager who had stolen her bag, the good- looking joe she 'd seen in Starbucks, and eventually, St. Johns.

Blink, blink, blink.

Darla was too stupefied to speak.

"Are we having delightful yet? " he said.

She realized her mouth was open. She closed it.

He chortled. " Sorry. I could n't repel. "

The meaning of it hit her. " You — you 're like me, " she said, her voice slightly above a tale.

"Yep. What you see is n't what you get, inescapably. "

He laughed again. " I do n't rob houses, my ambition is a little bigger than that, but I do okay. As you noticed when you spotted my cash box.

"How important did you take, by the way? "

"Two bills from each mound. "

"Smart. I like bright women. "

"Why are you — what —? "

"Well, I 've been watching you for a while, Darla. Far as I can tell you and I are the only two of our kind. I 'd propose a... cooperation. "

"Partnership? "

"Well. Further than that, perhaps. I mean, you're gorgeous and careful and clever, but there are some advantages to what we can do together. Between the two of us, we could do improved effects than either of us can do alone. Imagine how much easier it would be be if we could be a couple that looked like anybody we wanted? "

She considered it. Yes. That would be commodity.

"Plus there are some other gratuities. "

He lustered and turned into a studly youthful movie star that Darla much respected.

"Or perhaps... this? " He morphed into another youthful man, this one a match to a well-known gemstone star.

"We've a world of choice to offer each other, do n't we? " He lustered again, and reclaimed St. Johns. " Not that I suppose I would get wearied with you as you stand. You're stunning, you know, but you also have a kind of variety to offer no other woman does. "

She smiled back at him. " Indeed though I stole your plutocrat? "

"Because you stole my plutocrat. What do you suppose? "

She set up herself seesawing. Yes. There was an magnet, no question, and if she got tired of looking at him?

Well, he could fix that in an moment.

Because nothing was vulnerable to Glamour...

Chapter No. 7: The Policeman

You are a bobby. You knew that when you inked on. Be a damned good one.

EVERYBODY IN THE CITY KNOWS him. He's the harness bull who shoulders through the road crowd watching a fight and growls paternally, " each right! Break it up! Break it up! " He's the fellow leaning on the temptress as he pushes his black and white radio sport fisherman through red lights. He's the motor- bike man in white crash helmet intent on making life miserable for some taxpayer speeding down the highway.

He's the bobby.

Los Angeles is the place where that ridiculous calumniation on all police far and wide, the cornerstone Kop, was constructed. And like utmost metropolises, Los Angeles still feels a curious ambivalence toward the bobby. He gives protection, which is vaguely appreciated, but he also exercises authority which is begrudged if you admit the business ticket or court process.

So every stint the LAPD Policeman — progressed thirty- four, wedded, two children, paying for the house and auto on time has to prove himself again. " Bobbies are dogfaces who act alone, " notoriety formerly said, and each day the LAPD man in his lonely way must demonstrate his smarts, his heart, his guts.

Suddenly, on fancy Wilshire Boulevard, there are whoops and riots, and climbers scatter.

"What's the trouble? " Policeman George Audet growls. They tell him. A frenetic canine is loose, and formerly five persons have felt its bite.

Now it's up to Audet, and a thousand dyads of eyes are on him. It takes guts, but he has to do it. He unlimbers his gun and follows the salivating, ninety- pound beast into a yard, controlling him so there can be no escape for either of them. The frenetic beast tailbacks, tenses; and also, as he hops, Audet fires. He puts his slug coolly into the vital spot, and the beast drops dead.

Now the five victims must be rushed to a sanitarium, and business unsnarled. " All right, everybody. Move on. It's all over. "

On a Wednesday beforehand in June, Policemen William Morgan, motorist, and Nelson L. Brownson, guard, are moving nineteen captures in the command cart to the megacity jail. Suddenly, just as suddenly as a frenetic canine goes frantically, a machine carrying seventy-five children to a provincial academy near New Chinatown cuts off the cart.

Also the machine runs a red light, jumps the bridling, nearly hits a structure and crazily weaves back into the road again.

Morgan and Brownson give chase, adroitly drawing close alongside the swerving vehicle. It takes guts; a man could fall or get crushed; but Brownson hops into the machine, sprawling over the collapsed motorist. He manages to push him away and get the raw under control.

An ambulance is called for the diabetic motorist, who has gone into shock from an overdose of insulin.

"I do n't suppose the youths knew what was going on until it was each over, " Brownson says. " And they got to academy on time, too. "

But always, you come back to crime.

For some reason, August and December are hot months for burglary. It's August now, and Bobbies Gerald L. Bryan and Alvin L. Porterfield are pushing Unit 3A91 through the University Division on routine command.

As they cruise past a request, its alarm is ringing. A " 459, " radio law for burglary, is in progress. ordnance in hand, they probe.

Porterfield covers the front of the store. Bryan makes a quiet flanking approach to the reverse. Just as he's about to slip in the hinder door, he hears someone trying to open it from outside. He backs across the darkened alley into the murk along a concrete wall.

A perfect ambush. And also he freezes.

From alongside, on the other side of a rustic gate in the wall, he hears eleven low, cold words wrangle at him.

"Drop the gun, bobby— or die with it in your hand. "

Bryan takes a chance and steals a fast look. Not ten bases down, a lookout is gaping at him over the top of the gate, and the gun he holds is steady. The smart thing to do is to drop his own revolver.

Rather, Bryan suddenly bus and pours three shots into the gate. The gunfire brings Porterfield to his aid; and the coming moment they hear the crash of glass from the front of the store. Porterfield races back to the road, but the suspect has fled.

"Code 9, " he snaps into his radio mike in the sportfisherman auto. That's a call for backing.

Also he rejoins Bryan, and they find the lookout crumpled in a mound a many bases on the other side of the pellet- riddled gate. A loaded Walther P38 automatic is still in his hand, but he's too far gone to use it.

But before he dies, Bryan's quick questioning wins an admission of conspiracy and the identification of the abettor who got down. When backing arrives, there's not important to be done. See to it that a body is taken down and run down a name.

For the job, Bryan holds LAPD's Class A Commendation. That and twenty- five or thirty cents will buy a quart of milk at any store in city. He could have laid down his gun, avoided the awful threat, and his plutocrat would buy just as important milk moment.

That is n't the point. In the squadrooms, they say, "You're a bobby. You knew that when you inked on. Be a damned good bone. "

Always the unanticipated, and you play it hard and fast. also the awkward thing, the change of pace, just as unanticipated, but now you play it gently, compassionately.

The youthful mama is driving happily in the San Fernando Valley, her seven- months-old son alongside her. He's stinking on a slice of orange.

She ganders down tenderly, riots and thickets to a halt. A near radio auto pulls over to probe.

"No! " she screams hysterically. " You ca n't have my baby! "

All in a moment, he'd strangled to death on the orange. The bobbies snappily make sure the child is dead. She grabs the breathless form, leverages it, also drives off hectically with her dead baby.

Obediently, the radio auto follows, mothering her along the trace till she gets home. They give her a many twinkles to compose herself, and at last she realizes what has happed. Quietly, she hands over the limp form. They still see to it that family and neighbors are summoned to comfort her and also go on their way.

Give or take a many, there are some,590 men and 110 women who draw pay for the rank of bobby with LAPD. With their superior officers, they cover,000 long hauls of road in Los Angeles, operate,400 vehicles, and are outnumbered, five hundred to one, by the general crowd. The odds do n't feel relatively fair, and the LAPD Policeman tries to make up the difference with brain and body power.

He stands five bases ten elevation and weighs 165 to 170 pounds. He keeps in shape playing basketball or working out on the vertical bars.

He's a combat stager of either World War II or Korea. He still practices up on his firing. He serves in the military reserve on his own time. His Command is close to 120 (compared with the nation's normal of 100), and he's still going to council, on his own time. He's working toward a degree in Political Science or Public Administration.

On the normal, this sedately married, thirty- four- time-old father of two has been plugging along like this for seven times on the force. Curiously, he firstly came from out of state, and that's the only conception you can make about his mercenary background.

He may preliminarily have been a truck motorist, U.S. logger, clerk, lifeguard, plumber, salesperson, or indeed have studied for the priesthood or ministry before going on the force. He may have been a calculation major at council(with a 140 Command), who now rides a radio auto in the Valley.

He might indeed be the family of a Hollywood bookie; but he becomes an exemplary officer and lives as if there were no family.

Whatever he was, LAPD has reshaped and hardened him in its$,000 training earth, given him a essence emblem and put him out on the road where the bobby lives or dies.

"Be a damned good one, " the old- timekeepers tell him in the squad room.

Each stint, the unanticipated.

Day, and Policeman Eugene R. Crammer Jr. is routinely directing autumn rush- hour business at a town crossroad. There's a cry for help, and Crammer, unlimbering his gun as he picks his way through the hurrying buses , makes for the scene.

In ten twinkles, he has disarmed two markswomen and transferred them off to Central reserving for tried thievery.

Nighttime and Bobbies C.J. Chapman and R.J. Brown are cruising on Hollywood Boulevard at 347a.m. They're learning the rearmost addition to "the hot distance," the license number of an nearly-new sports auto stolen from a road in Hollywood.

At Hollywood Boulevard and Cherokee Avenue, just twenty- five twinkles after the report was made, they spot the fast, candescent bug. They give chase, and for three long hauls through the heart of Hollywood, they slue round corners at shocking speed.

In a way, it's ironic. There are,194 road corners in LAPD's home, and Chapman and Brown know them all, or utmost all. But at DeLongpre Avenue and Cahuenga Boulevard, just a loud yell from the Hollywood Division, there's a unfaithful dip in the road.

Unfaithful, anyhow, for a auto thundering at their speed. They spin out of control, slam into two situated buses and escape, ever, with just nasty cuts and bruises. They lose the bug, but their threat does n't go in vain.

Thirty twinkles latterly, while they're being darned up at the sanitarium, other bobbies

find the sports auto situated back exactly where it had been taken. But Chapman and Brown had given the pincher such a dread that he accidentally dropped an identification card outside.

He's arrested and confesses. Chapman and Brown go home. Their women recoil at the sight of the tapes, and all they can say is, " It was a little rough tonight, honey. But nothing serious. Nothing for you to worry about. "

Occasionally, in the smooth way of ultramodern police, it's a triadic play. During a tricky heart operation in a stagers ' sanitarium, a extremity suddenly developed. The surgeon demanded fresh outfit, and he demanded it presto, to keep the white- faced case alive. The only place the outfit could be attained was at Good Samaritan Hospital, and that involved a thirty- five afar trip.

In relays, Bobbies L.S. Rasic, Charles Cunningham and Lawrence Berdlow got it and got it back to the stagers ' sanitarium, passing it on from one to the other each in 35 twinkles. Risking their lives at better than afar-a-minute speed, they saved another.

Too frequently, just because of the miserable nature of the job, it's still the lonesome one-man operation it always was for an officer before the bus and radio were constructed. They tell him where to go and get him there presto, and that's all they can do. He's alone with a dirty, dangerous bone.

It's near the end of his long, hot day's stint, and though the July sun has slanted down in the west, the temperature still stands at 92. Patrolling all day in the western end of the San Fernando Valley, Policeman Paul Cleary has just about had it.

It's been the kind of day when the clayish soil of the West Valley gets as hard as asphalt and the asphalt softens to the thickness of complexion. Cleary wants to get under a needle-cold wave shower, get a good cold drink.

"Law 3"

The alarm — exigency; red light and temptress — shakes him out of his languor. He listens, and his name is tied to it.

"Debris on the road tracks one hundred yards west of Lindley. Train due at 520p.m. "

Cleary ganders at his watch. It's 515.

The radio sends him and the sport fisherman gets him there and now he's back on his own. It's 518p.m. snappily he ganders up and down the tracks. He sees nothing, and the affable words, " Report unsupported, " come into his mind. He looks again and a good 400 yards out, west toward the hills that skirt the Valley, he sees commodity.

He starts running in loose, easy strides, trying to pace himself. One hundred yards two hundred yards. He's half home now, and he ought to make it.

Also he hears the train whoosh.

Sweat pouring down his back, he runs at full speed now. He finds the inhibition, two lengths of pipe, two elevation by five bases, and an old truck tire. They've been jammed on and between the rails.

The San Francisco Limited, highballing into Los Angeles from the seacoast, thunders into view. Desperately, Cleary claws at the pipe and tire as the train bears down on him. He pulls them clear, nearly falling backward, and the train sweeps safely by.

Be a damned good one.

In LAPD, as in utmost big metropolises, the radio auto command man is the departmental torpedo which can be fired from Headquarters, incontinently and in any direction, in response to trouble. The men drive further than six million long hauls yearly. Every twelve seconds there's a new transmission over their auto radio.

But a torpedo, or a submarine, is wasted unless it hits the target. Every LAPD radio man has to settle the exigency or at least wage a holding operation till his law 9 (Request for backing) can be answered. Then, unlike numerous metropolises, the radio man operates alone, rather than in dyads, during the day command.

Actually, this calculated threat was forced on LAPD by a force deficit. By unyoking up the two- man radio brigades in all geographical divisions, the police doubled their day content. The move was made cautiously after field tests in tough and soft neighborhoods and drastic training variations to educate the bobbies how to fight a one- man fight. also LAPD's heads crossed their fritters and awaited.

In the first time of single operation, assaults against police officers dropped some 20 (from 124 to 99), felony apprehensions increased slightly, and misdemeanor apprehensions were over by further than one- third. LAPD had won.

Curiously, nothing can say for sure why it has worked out. Some give the credit to the men themselves. They know they're on their mettle; and they know the fellow on the coming beat is alone and on his mettle, too. By radio, they follow his conditioning, and when the going gets rough, they move by fast to cover him.

Hearteningly, the servicewoman has come through to help one beleaguered officer where he might not help a platoon. Police reports now list scores of incidents in which citizen backing has reduced complaint and prevented injury to the officer at the scene of a crime.

LAPD appreciates the benevolence.

Before all the road exertion, disconnected though it may feel as the radio buses siren off in colorful directions, there's a directing voice.

Without talk, ultramodern police departments just could n't serve, especially one like LAPD with such an enormous ground area to cover. Its voice, a massive electronic and wireless network of teletype and shortwave radio, covers not only Los Angeles but also can be projected throughout California.

In the Dispatches Division, the sixty- six sworn labor force are supplemented by eighty-five radio telephone drivers, plus another fifteen in the teletype and communication sections. A separate unit, the Radio Technical Division, keeps thirty- eight civilians busy, operating the main receivers and transmitters and maintaining the intricate outfit.

Through the combined sweats of dispatchers, drivers, and technicians, LAPD's potent voice can be heard in further than 800 two- way mobile units, some forty three- way mobile units which can talk auto- to- auto, further than twenty walkie- pictures and about fifty stationary receivers.

There's noway a frog in its throat. That would be as disastrous, perhaps more so, as a police department without a gun. Four main transmitters, spotted strategically throughout the megacity, are aided by two movable transmitters for extremities and one fully mobile command station.

Also, LAPD maintains transmitters and receivers forinter-city andinter-state dispatches with police away. These handle radiograms for all Southern California law enforcement agencies, and a sixty- machine teletype system connects in with all county seats and major police agencies far and wide in California.

The good old days of outriding the cortege to safety in the coming county are gone ever!

Every nanosecond of the twenty- four hours, the complaint switchboard is lighted with calls, and the bobbies - drivers must make their opinions on the spot. What does LAPD roll on? What is trivial and pointless?

A complaint about a situated auto blocking a driveway? Not insignificant if a croaker is thereby averted from making his rounds. The o- so-familiar complaint about a barking canine? Not insignificant if maybe the canine is barking because his master is dead. The decision must be made fast, the taxpayer gently treated.

" To every citizen, his call is important, " explains one driver. " occasionally all he wants is to talk to notoriety, to cry on notoriety's shoulder. We offer him the shoulder. "

At 417p.m., the board suddenly receives a report about a store in the Wilshire District. There's no mistrustfulness that LAPD will roll on this bone.

A little white form reporting law 2 (critical; no red light, temptress) goes on the conveyor to the dispatch room for instant transmission. A torpedo is fired.

420p.m. The " hot shot " phone, reserved for exigency calls, chimes beside the master control board. The radio auto officer is formerly reporting back from the scene. It's a " 211, " a thievery, and he needs help.

Law 2 becomes Code 3 (exigency; red light, temptress) and further torpedoes are launched.

Now Dispatches sweats it out. Will still further help be needed? What redundant units are available and how close are they?

429p.m. The " hot shot " phone rings again. Suspect restrained, situation under control exactly twelve twinkles after the first alert. All units return to normal command.

LAPD addresses substantially in a cropped, number law not for purposes of secretiveness but for quicker transmission and conservation of air time. With five to six calls going out every nanosecond, each word is important, and " Code 1 " is vastly lower longwinded than " Admit Your Call. "

There's a number for nearly every contingency from " Code 7, " Out to Eat, to the dreaded "Code 13 Daniel, " which is a disaster calling in all off- duty officers, reserves, and auxiliaries. Plain figures like "211" for thievery and " 484 " for theft indicate the specific crime involved by its section under the California Penal Code.(The full Radio law is published at the end of this chapter.)

The apothecary on the phone with the complaint board is hysterical. He's soliciting LAPD to save a woman's life.

Two days before, he'd made up a tradition calling for dilantin. rather, by mistake, he'd used a digitalis medication. He has just discovered his mistake — a conceivably fatal mistake, because if the woman follows the lozenge specified on the bottle, she'll die in about eight days.

From the blubbing man, the police gain the tradition number; and in the coming partial hour, they negotiate this important The tradition is traced to General Hospital, where it had been issued three months before by a staff croaker. The sanitarium gives a name and an address in East Los Angeles. The woman, it's set up, had moved from there some two months preliminarily. No forwarding address.

But investigators establish that she's of Mexican descent, thirty- four times old, five bases one inch, 115 pounds, red- haired. They find she has been known under three names and learn the whereabouts of her mama and other cousins.

Again, no luck. The mama explains that she infrequently sees her son, and the other cousins ca n't help.

Now the only stopgap of saving a woman's life is a citywide hunt. Chief of investigators Thad Brown incontinently authorizes use of all LAPD's installations.

Every command is advised, all jails and hospitals notified, a teletype flashed throughout Los Angeles County. Under Captain Stanley H. Sheldon, the department's public relations unit appeals to journals, radio and television to publicize the warning.

A Sigalert bulletin is drafted; and every quarter hour the megacity's radio stations, which between them reach into three countries and Mexico, make this advertisement

Attention This is a Sigalert reprise. The Los Angeles Police Department states that anyone knowing Josephine Aguilar, also known as Josephine Sandez, also known as Josephine Sanchez, please advise her incontinently that the tradition she had filled on February 16, between 630p.m. and 7p.m. at a apothecary in the southern part of Los Angeles, was inaptly compounded. It contains a largely dangerous medicine, which could beget her death.

Anyone knowing this lady should report her whereabouts to 77th Street investigators, Madison 4- 5211, Extension 2618.

R. Selby —Lt. Lindsay Simmons

Ticket# 8- 289

In just three diggings of an hour after the apothecary's frantic call, the investigators ' phones are hopelessly jammed with the public response. The flood tide of incoming dispatches must be incompletely diverted to the invariant unit and nearly anyone with an extension, including Juvenile.

People who flash back once having employed a Josephine Aguilar leave their homes at night and go back to the office to search old records for an address or phone number. Physicians and dentists who had treated cases of that name call in. musketeers of the woman levy to help. Other Josephine Aguilars call to say they're each right and do n't desolate time looking for them. Just, please, find that poor woman before it's too late!

There is commodity heart- warming in the way the public responds so incontinently to a call for help. Indeed toughened LAPD men are impressed, and yet with all the calls, nothing is fulfilled. The woman is still missing.

During the night, the flood tide of incoming dispatches falls to a teardrop, and also at 8a.m., the switchboard lights up again. Everyone in the county, it seems, knows a Josephine Aguilar.

Eventually, a little after nine, a woman's voice announces that she's the Josephine Aguilar.

Yes, she's the one who had the tradition filled. No, no, she's each right.

Right down, after getting them, she had noticed the capsules were the wrong size and color, not like the bones ahead. So she just had n't taken any of them.

Where is she now? Calling from a phone cell near her mama 's home.

When she got up this morning, she turned on her radio to a Spanish- language program. The host was talking about a big hunt for a woman with the same name. But she did n't realize it was she herself till her mama 's name and address also were broadcast. She got dressed and went to mamma's to tell her she was each right.

Yes, she'd meet the investigators in ten twinkles and give them the bad bottle.

In lower than ten twinkles, investigators are at the door, and Josephine hands over the deadly capsules.

Be a damned good one.

At the wheel, he's perhaps a drunk or just a sprat showing off for his girl. Whoever he is, he's hanging every living thing in his path as he roars past the situated motorcycle officer at ninety long hauls an hour. In the dark, it's delicate to see a license plate at sixty bases. At his speed, he's passing the officer at 135 bases a alternate.

With his right hand opening the throttle, his left clinging the radio microphone, the officer takes after him.

"4 Mary 105 is in pursuit, " he says matter of factly to Dispatches. That means a hustler is being chased in the Hollenbeck police division.

Snappily Dispatches comes on the air.

"All frequentness stand by. Mary 105 is in pursuit. "

To avoid an air jumble, all broadcast ceases on the band. Other units stay for a pattern to develop so they can meet.

"Outbound Santa Ana Freeway, " Mary 105 now reports. " Pursuit ' 58 Olds. "

Also silence.

Astride a 55- power Harley Davidson, Mary 105 is now straining against the wind at one hundred long hauls an hour, trying to close the gap between him and the 265 power Olds.

At that speed on a little bike, he's living, second to second, only by the grace of God. The blast of wind in his cognizance cuts off all other sound. He's at the mercy of the road, its angles, indeed a small gravestone. He could n't stop suddenly, though his life might hang at the coming turn on a quick stop.

He has n't had time to slip on his spectacles, and the wind rakes his eyeballs. He sees only space roaring toward him and a dwindling white line that gashes beneath his left bottom.

Everything additional, trees, houses, gravestone walls, are a pointless blur. Light is shadow, and shadow is a black smear in the cobalt. also a tail light ahead winks redder as the hustler thickets and eventually stops.

The motor officer pulls alongside. For a many seconds, as he unwinds, he has a bad case of the shakes. He fights for tone- control, also says unevenly to the alarmed teenager, " each right, gentleman. Let's see the license and enrollment . "

A fast pursuit by motorcycle is one of the most dangerous and draining of all police gests. Relatively directly, LAPD calls its motorbike force the " Iron horsemen. "

Unexpectedly, despite the fire, there are always scores of Bobbies on the waiting list hoping for a chance to join the Traffic Enforcement Division. Riding a bike can mean as important as$ 50 further per month, but that's the least part of it.

The norms for acceptance are challengingly high, the morale is superb, and TED is a flashy, spit- and- polish unit.

Its twenty- five man motor fraternity drill platoon has won the public American Legion crowns, and there's a proud jauntiness about TED that makes a man forget his own neck some of the time.

Only Bobbies with at least one time's experience are eligible for the transfer. Those tentatively accepted also suffer a series of emphatic sickie-physical aptitude tests. After that, they must pass an oral examination before ranking TED officers, labor force, and command, which is double- checked by the Chief of labor force and two inspectors.

That is n’t all.

There's a tough two- weeks ’ course in riding academy and a training course in business enforcement and procedure, during which each neophyte is under constant observation.

Is he a throttle- snapper or a hot rodder? He washes out. TED wants cautious courage, not recklessness, much the same norms set for our military birdmen.

Eventually, he must be a gentleman because he'll ride out to vend commodity that nothing really wants — business enforcement.

The records and colorful spot checks expose that TED does vend enforcement. Only one in a hundred motorists tries to give the “Iron horseman ” an argument when he's marked. The other ninety- nine accept the paper courteously, or at least resignedly.

Before going on their individual watches, the “Iron horsemen” congregate at the Police erecting for roll call. There they are posted on the diurnal orders and any changes in procedures, briefed on unusual late crime that may affect them.

Also, typical of their tight morale, they informally put heads together to hash over what they call “frinstance cases, ” theoretical situations which might just arise eventually and bear special running.

Still, they're given a reprieve from bike riding and temporarily assigned to Accident Investigation or clearances, If the rainfall is stormy. But if it's clear, they stand at attention by their bikes, distrustfully smelling the air for signs of gauze, also mount in accord and leave in smart, military conformation.

With a loud, proud roar from his little 55- hp motor, each “Iron horseman ” peels off in turn for his own beat, which has been determined for him on base of senility. There's no favoritism in TED, and at the end of any month, an officer without “ enough whiskers ” can be banged from his beat by an officer who outranks him and wants to change.

No officer can indeed guess what the day’s command will bring ahead he signs off, “ 139, end of watch. ”

Officer S.W. Combs was shocked and outraged one day to discover a nineteen- time-old North Hollywood youth driving one hand on the highway — and he did n’t have the other arm around a girl, moreover. He was paring with an electric razor. Setting a new enforcement precedent, Combs cited him for reckless driving.

Responding to a law 3 (exigency; red light, temptress), Officer Dale Phillips set up that an unconventional bank purloiner had made his flight in a hack. Just as unconventionally, Phillips on his bike, rather than a radio sport fisherman, captured the hack, internee, spoil, munitions, and all.

Any time an “Iron horseman ” overhauls a business violator, there's a quick, tense size up. The man behind the wheel may be just a careless motorist and also again he might be a miscreant.

Formerly, when Officer Fud Denny flagged down a auto that had made a wrong lane turn, the motorist convincingly flashed a bright new driver’s license which indicated emotional past driving experience in Europe. Commodity smelled wrong to the officer.

Questioning the man more nearly, Denny set up that he did n’t know the first thing about Los Angeles business laws. He detained him while Motor Vehicles ran a fast check.

The driver’s license, DMV reported, had been fraudulently attained, and a farther check bared the automobilist had immorally jumped a foreign boat also docked in Los Angeles. He was handed over to the immigration authorities.

Of course, motorists being motorists, some effects are just bound to be again and again, the "Iron horsemen " know resignedly. For case, though they handle the wheel more, the men motorists are going to give the bike man further trouble than women motorists. Say what you'll about that woman motorist, it's the man who does the most speeding and commits the most deliberate violations. That's the verity.

The highway is a more rugged watch than the " face thoroughfares "; that is, those off the highway. Everything, anything can be on the highway, and the " Iron horseman " nearly gets cross-eyed watching for dalliers, creepers, tail riders and unsafe lane changers, not to mention truck and caravan violations and a many revealed loads then and there.

Whatever his beat, he's charged with administering all laws and bills regulating business. Since enforcement has to be picky because of the small size of TED, the motor bike man is stationed in the area where accidents are occurring. However, he tails business for a stretch, watching for the malefactors, If inside end has been causing the trouble. However, he premises on a lateral road till some Oldfield pets by, If it's speed.

Rule o' thumb, the motorcycle police consider the " normal inflow of business " in judging speed. Depending on the road, time, and rainfall, this is an elastic rule which can be stretched from fifteen mph to fifty- five and indeed more.

Since a man could n't conceivably write all the business violations he spots during an eight- hour watch, general enforcement has to be optional, too. He picks out the stylish — or, rather, the worst — of them for tickets.

"There are no hard and fast rules, " says Fred McGrew. " We just put ourselves in the motorist's shoes. "

Officer Frederick J. McGrew, age 37, six bases one and a half elevation altitudinous, 195 pounds in weight, a stager of the U.S. Armored Tank service, is one of TED's most imposing business- law clerks. He draws further than average pay and has the honor of riding his bike to and from work. (All LAPD motorcycle officers take their bikes home to assure the department a ready, mobile force, if demanded.)

But he has redundant costs, too. While the department kindly furnishes his white crash helmet, his livery, including thrills, costs further than$ 100, and his leather jacket stands him$ 55. His gun represents another$ 75 investment; and, in addition, at varied prices to him, he totes a chain and whoosh, Sam Brown belt, bind, cane holder, security case, gloves, flashlight, companion book, "hot distance " holder, cane, and pen. Also his emblem and book of business citations. Fortunately, the ultimate two particulars do n't represent important fresh weight, and they come free, courtesy of the Los Angeles Police Department.

At the end of two weeks, McGrew's take- home pay is$156.55. But he's paying levies and pretenses to the Police Protective League and the American Legion. He's making payments on pension, insurance, and auto. He's buying a house and bringing up two children. He rides a tight budget.

And like every other " Iron horseman, " he noway knows what the coming watch will bring. One night, McGrew and a mate were riding the night watch — 8p.m.- to- 4a.m. — in a smart business-domestic quarter. They rode that way by night in the motor fraternity, in tandem, one hand helping the other. It was a lazy night. The drunks were home, or had n't yet left the bars, and the dalliers were n't hitting this area.

At 1230a.m., as the officers were passing a marketable crossroad, a man ran out of a large food store, signaling frenetically to them. He was the store director, he explained, and he'd returned a short while ahead to check the books. There had been strange noises someone was in there right now!

Ordnance in hand, McGrew and his mate accompanied the director outside. They turned on the lights and, in one office; set up the safe door had been smashed open, supposedly by a meat cleaver, which lay hard. But the sizable weekend bills hadn't been disturbed.

Obviously, they figured, the meddler had been spooked off by the director, but presumably had n't had the time to escape. Counter by counter, they searched the request, poked into corners and demurred the big food boxes piled then and there.

McGrew demurred one box, and it did n't move. " All right, " he snapped. " Come out presto. " A head and also a hand clinging a.45 surfaced sluggishly. McGrew transferred the automatic spinning and collared his man.

The meddler, who was employed in another store of the same food chain, knew the weekend bills would be heavy and knew the employer's routine. He'd buried himself in the store till everybody left about 10p.m. and also had gone to work on the safe with his meat cleaver. Just as his assiduity had eventually paid off two and a half hours latterly, the director had returned.

It's not like that every watch, but indeed a comparatively quiet eight hours on the highway leaves McGrew bushed. Indeed without trouble, he has ridden 200 long hauls, and he's pleased to radio his " 139. "

McGrew also bikes home, does a little gardening, fools around with the kiddies for awhile and eventually goes off into a room alone to work on his hobbyhorse. nights, McGrew draws cartoons and sells them to the magazines.

Always, you come back to crime.

You play it hard and fast and cagey. A bobby's payment wo n't cover a verdict for false arrest.

Beforehand on a spring morning, Bobbies Robert Coffman and Jack Carter are working the night watch out of Central Division. At 126a.m., a 459 sends them to the apartment structure at 251 Loma Drive, and the night's fun begins.

Returning from a show, a couple find their apartment has been completely pillaged. Clothing, linen, books, and film land are bestrew about; closets and snuggeries have been voided. About$, 700 worth of jewelry and apparel are missing.

To the police, the system of entry is egregious. The burglar placed a scrap can near the hinder bedroom window, climbed atop it, also cut the screen, pried open the window, and entered.

But one thing bothers them. On the living room table,$ 70 in cash is lying in plain view. Why did n't he take it?

Either he did n't see it, which does n't make important sense, considering his thoroughness, or the couple's return spooked him off. In that case, he might still be around the neighborhood.

Carter remains in the apartment to get a description of the missing property, and Coffman scouts the neighborhood. On the parkway, near a situated auto, he finds pieces of a broken piggy bank. He brings them back, and the victim's woman identifies them.

Now a DMV (Department of Motor Vehicles) license hunt discloses that the auto is registered to a woman in Sherman Oaks, a good distance down. The auto seems worth as take out. However, he should come back for it, If the burglar used it.

For an hour, also two, and eventually three hours, Carter and Coffman watch the auto. Just before dawn, they're ready to give up. But they 've wasted three hours; and they may as well sit tight another partial hour till it's good and light.

In a many further twinkles, a man rounds the corner, passes the apartment house without a regard at it and heads toward the auto. The officers hold back. perhaps he's a poker player coming home late or a joe just off the graveyard shift. Let's stay a nanosecond.

Near the situated auto, the man looks about cautiously, also walks up and snappily unlocks the door. From a hundred bases down the road, Coffman comes pounding toward him.

For a moment, the suspect seems about to take off, but Coffman is on him. He gives him a quick shake for a gun, also asks his name.

"Arthur John Stark. "

"You're up enough late, are n't you? "

"I 'm old enough. I guess forty- eight is old enough. "

Mr. Stark does n't understand this routine at all. He has noway been arrested in his life, and he does n't like this kind of treatment. What does Coffman suppose he is, a felonious or commodity?

Coffman stalls a moment. The auto, Mr. Stark?

Belongs to a friend, Mr. Stark explains fluently, and he has just espoused it for the night. Anything wrong about that?

Coffman chews it over. The answer is stroke and yet ever a bit fugitive. Mr. Stark's good-citizen bluster seems a bit uneasy. But the move is over to the officer. If he takes him in and Mr. Stark is pure, there 'll be hell to pay.

Coffman studies the auto, looks into the aft seat. It's covered with apparel.

"You 'll have to come town, Mr. Stark, " he says still.

Stark is reserved in Central Jail on dubitation

of burglary, and Coffman sweats it out while the Burglary Division runs a make on Mr. Stark. He's far, far from pure.

Beginning at the age of nineteen, and that goes back to the Twenties, Mr. Stark has been in trouble. In Michigan, Oregon, Nevada, and California. He has done time in San Quentin and Folsom incarcerations.

A report comes in on the auto he'd " espoused " from a friend. It's stolen.

Stark was condemned of burglary on May 3, 1956, and transferred to San Quentin as a two- time clunker.

Be a damned good one.

Sure, you 'd had two or three beers, but that was n't what caused it. The big, arrogant white Cadillac cut the corner sharp, forcing you to smack into a situated auto. The Caddy keeps going, and when the radio sport fisherman shows up, there you're each alone, with a broken tulle on your auto.

Excitedly you tell the Bobbies what happed. Being angry, you talk a little too loud, and maybe you gesture your arms. One of the officers wrinkles his nose. " You been drinking, Mac "

"Two or three beers, " you say belligerently. " What has that got to do with being cut off! "

The Bobbies change ganders. noway, in police history, has it been four or five beers. noway, noway further than two or three beers.

"Suppose I 'm drunk, " you say. " Look! "

You touch your cutlet to your nose. One of the officers has gone back to make a radio call, and, drawing an imaginary line to the police auto, you walk it straight toward him. Or nearly straight, anyhow.

"Take it easy, Mac, " says his mate. " AID will be right then. "

In no time, an Accident Investigation auto swings up beside the sport fisherman. There's a little talk among the bobbies, and also the AID man comes over to you, carrying a narrow, ten- inch-long cardboard cylinder.

He takes out a balloon and a couple of glass tubes which have some kind of chemicals outside. He hands you the balloon and says, " Go ahead, blow into it. "

"What's this! "

"Go ahead, blow. We 're taking a sample of your breath. "

You vacillate distrustfully. It's a trap.

"What are you hysterical of? You only had two or three beers, did n't you? "

So you exhale into the balloon. He snappily turns a mouth stopcock to trap the breath outside, and also he runs the breath into one of the glass tubes. " This is for the lab, " he says. " Now blow again. "

The alternate time, he runs the breath into the other tube. It mixes with some chemicals, and there seems to be a faint abrasion. " We 'll have to check town, Mac, " he says.

Now you begin to sweat. You did have only two or three beers. The big Caddy did cut you off, but nothing saw it. Your whole case rests in two little glass tubes.

You go on with the officers, and you really sweat it out, staying for the lab report. Eventually, one of the radio men comes out of a reverse room at Headquarters.

"Take it easy, Mac," he says. " Like you said, it was only two or three beers. Now, are you sure you did n't get indeed part of the Caddy's license number"

For the exculpation, which presumably saved you from a "502" conviction as a crapulous motorist, you can thank a enough youthful policewoman. Chestnut- haired, brown- eyed Geraldine Lambert, woman of an LAPD assistant, is one of the many policewoman forensic judges in the country.

A graduate of the University of California at Los Angeles, Geraldine began her career as an logical druggist with the Eastman Kodak Processing Laboratory. When she came a police woman, she broke in the usual way with juvenile and jail assignments and a hitch in DAPs, or Deputy Auxiliary Police, the departmental youth group.

For nearly a decade now, she has been in the Crime Lab, learning the fascinating complications of blood analysis under LAPD's principal druggist, Ray Pinker. She has been one of the two women chosen to serve on the Chemical Test Committee of the National Safety Council, and has been suggested "Policewoman of the Time " by the Exchange Club of Los Angeles.

At a cost of further than$,000 for constituents alone, Geraldine packs,000 chemical " In oximeter " accoutrements a time. Not all return. Of the drunks that annually fill the balloons with reflective whisked breaths, some,200 maintain shamefaced and avert the need of In oximeter analysis.

But 800 a time dispute the drunk charge. Also the fine eye of wisdom draws a blob on the data. The In oximeter tells the story.

Occasionally the indicted is right. occasionally he loses. The Intoximeter cost to the megacity, LAPD knows, is further than worth it, not only in nailing down some " 502 " persuasions, but in clearing the innocent.

Frequently motorists in ill health like diabetics fail the field sobriety tests. Geraldine clears them. And occasionally defendants on other charges try to act drunk to alleviate their offenses. Geraldine's chemistry exposes the chicane. Whatever she finds, her evidence is nearly always accepted by the courts.

The breath sample turned over to the Crime Lab is measured for the proportion of alcohol in the bloodstream. Magnesium perchlorate chargers in the Intoximeter tube have trapped the alcohol which is first brume- distilled and measured for volume. By relating the volume to the volume of breath taken as a sample, the proportion of alcohol in the bloodstream is caught on. In turn, this can be restated into degrees of drunkenness.

Therefore, your two or three beers might leave a trace of alcohol in the bloodstream. But so long as you run under.05 per cent on the test, you're chemically sober, and the courts will so agree.

From.05 to.10 per cent indicates that the subject has been drinking;.10 to.15 you're conceivably under the influence of alcohol. From.15 to.25, you're under the influence of liquor and shouldn't be driving. At.25 per cent you're obviously intoxicated; at.35 per cent you're a common drunk and presumably unfit to take care of yourself; and at.40 per cent, whether you're apprehensive of it or not, you have passed out.

Beyond that, the probabilities begin to indicate a grim prognostic. At.50 per cent, you have imbibed a murderous quantum of good fellowship.

Occasionally, Geraldine's teacups and burners forestall an indecorous booking. There was, for illustration, the known San Pedro alcoholic, set up one night drooped behind the wheel of his situated auto. He was out cold.

It would have been the most egregious thing in the world to bespeak him as a drunk. rather, the officers awakened him and made him take the Intoximeter test.

Geraldine's report was an eye- nature. His blood alcohol position was only.02 per cent! farther disquisition bared the alcoholic had gulped a vial of paraldehyde in an trouble to avoid the DTs.

On another occasion, a hubby beat his woman to death in their home in San Fernando Valley and also fled over the hill into Hollywood. Furnished with his description, investigators fluently picked him up. Too fluently, it sounded to them. He was set up staggering through the thoroughfares, a half-empty wine bottle in his fund, and, indeed if he had n't been wanted for murder, he'd have been bagged as a drunk.

The investigators instantly called for an AID auto to give him the Intoximeter test. He proved out at .07 per cent, just possible drunkenness.

latterly at his trial, the man tried to maintain that he'd been drunk and did n't know what he was doing when he killed his woman. The State also introduced the Intoximeter finding, and he was condemned.

Further and further, police throughout the nation are using scientific chemical tests for intoxication, but LAPD is formerly testing another device which may prove to be both simpler and cheaper. While it uses chemicals, as does the Intoximeter, renewals are only sixty cents against$2.50. The instrument can be used at the booking office or indeed plugged into the cigarette fighter of a police auto, and you do n't need a druggist to read the results. The device feeds the breath past a photoelectric cell and snaps a picture of the breath content, which can be used in court.

In a way, there's an applicable irony in the new, quiet kind of operative work that Geraldine Lambert and Ray Pinker pursue far from the scene of a crime or crapulous-motorist accident. These malefactors haven't dithered to slip blood, and by blood they're betrayed.

A .25 per cent reading in the bloodstream can not be concealed; the blood- soaked handkerchief of a killer can be washed white, and yet, under Pinker's benzidine test, there will be a ruinous, blue-green chemical response. The shamefaced can adulterate blood,000 times, and still Pinker will find it.

So far as wisdom knows, blood is virtually imperishable through age. It has been set up in the gist of Egyptian corpses several thousand times old. It's nearly always there to point to a miscreant.

Out, out, damned spot. But it'll not out.

Always, you come back to crime. And the road.

That's where the bobby lives, fights, occasionally dies.

In the Wilmington area down by the harbor, Policeman Dallas W. Walters, Harbor Division clearances Detail, has just come out of a store. Three fortified goons compass him.

It's a burglary, and the smart thing is to let them have his plutocrat, his gun, his emblem.

Walters fights.

It's three- to- one, and he catches three slugs, one in each leg and the third in the shoulder. He goes down, but he's still shooting. He kills one bandit and critically injuries the alternate.

The odds are indeed now; so the third drags his wounded companion into a auto and runs.

In no time, nine officers in four buses have reached the scene, but everybody has gone except Walters lying in the road and his kill hard. One radio auto follows the ambulance that takes the poorly wounded officer to the sanitarium, and there's a little reunion in exigency. The wounded marksman had been dropped there by his confidante. Latterly, the third man is set up hiding in the box of the escape auto.

Walters recovers, and only now and also, substantially in stormy rainfall, do the old injuries pain. He's satisfied.

As they say in the squad rooms, " Be a damned good bone. "

Occasionally, because women and children are in the crossfire, you play it soft, pianissimo, and just as dangerously.

"Al, this is Dee. "

"What! "

"Dee. Dee Lightner. The bobby. "

The phone is suddenly silent.

"Al! I 'm telephoning from hard. "

"Stay a nanosecond "

"The place is girdled, Al. I want you to come out and surrender. "

"Give me a chance! I got ta suppose. "

"You can take it the easy way. Or the hard way. "

"What do you want me to do? "

"I 'm coming up after you. Up to the door. When I ring the bell, shove your gun through the door and you follow it. Hands behind your head. "

"Okay, okay. "

The phone goes silent again.

"Come on, Al. I mean it. I said it's a deal. "

"Okay. But do n't let them shoot me. Please! Do n't shoot me! "

"You do it right, Al, and nothing will shoot you. "

The phone clicks dead.

Police officer De Witt C. Lightner comes out of the cell. "He said okay, " he tells the FBI agent staying there. They look speculatively at each other. " Let's stopgap he means it, " the G- man says.

Together, they drive a block to Firebird Avenue in Whittier, east of Los Angeles. They situate across the road from the seedy little frame house where badman Albert J. Kostal is drilled up.

Kostal is unfaithful and quick on the detector. He's wanted for thievery and maybe two murders. Eleven days before, he'd busted out of an eighth- bottom detention pen of the Los Angeles Hall of Justice, taking two musketeers with him.

The musketeers were snappily caught, but Al had remained at large till an anonymous, early morning tip to the FBI had located his den. Now all police agencies in the Los Angeles area have blocked off the quarter. They're going to take Al the easy way or dig him out with shotgun, dynamo, and triadic- chaser.

But there are women, perhaps children, in the little frame house, and Dee Lightner offers his plan. He knows Al enough well, having returned him from Kansas City to Los Angeles just a many months before as an escapee from Folsom, the outside- security captivity.

Al was doing life, and now the state's clerks are calculating how much more he owes for his two escapes. It's a lot to ask a man like that to hand out his gun, buttfirst. However, he might shoot Dee and try a break, If he decides to play the long odds. Or make him run hindrance as a guard. Or yank him inside as a hostage.

Five twinkles after the phone call, Dee Lightner walks across the silent, vacated road, walks up the path and onto the veranda , presses the doorbell. There's no answer.

Outside, Al hears him, each right, but he wants to try a last escapade.

He runs to the aft door, hoping he can reach his flight auto stockpiled in the garage. He opens it, and four shotguns are raised against him. He hesitates in the doorway.

From behind the garage, a small child wanders uncertainly across the line of fire. Now, Al!

But a sheriff's officer jumps out, pushes the boy to safety and regains cover. That breaks Al. sluggishly he walks back outside and goes to the frontal door.

He opens it, hands his gun to Dee Lightner. He comes out, hands behind his head.

Be a damned good one.

But always, you come back to crime. And the road. TED Officer Michael J. McAndrews was safe and off duty in his own home when it happen.

McAndrews was recovering from a bout with the flu, and the croaker had advised him, "Take it easy, boy. This thing is unfaithful. "

"Sure," Mike had said. "Do n't worry, Doc. I 'll take it easy. "

And also it happed right outside his own window. A sprat crashed a auto, a stolen auto, it developed latterly, and McAndrews saw him fleeing. Two deputy sheriffs were chasing him on bottom.

It's always the bobby's job to help. McAndrews joined the chase and though it winded him poorly, he caught the sprat. He held him till the deputies took over. And Officer Michael J. McAndrews dropped dead of a heart attack.

Yes, like they say, be a damned good one.

Chapter No. 8: Someday I'll Plant More Walnut Trees

There's a silence that's just stillness, just the absence of sound, and there's a deeper silence that's further than that. It's the antipode, the aggressive contrary, of sound. It's to sound as antimatter is to count, an audile black hole that reaches out to swallow up and abate the sounds of others.

My mama can give off such a silence. She's a master at it. That morning at breakfast she was therefore silent, silent as she cooked eggs and made coffee, silent while I laded baby oatmeal into Livia's little mouth, silent while Dan fed himself and while he smoked the day's first cigarette along with his coffee. He'd his own silence, sitting there behind his review, but all it did was isolate him. It could n't reach out beyond that paper guard to catch other sound out of the air.

He finished and put out his cigarette, folded his paper. He said it was supposed to be hot moment, with rain cast for late autumn. He gentled Livia's head, and with his forefinger drew away a beachfront of hair that had fallen across her forepart.

I can see that now, his hand so gentle, and her beaming up at him, wide- eyed, goggling.

Also he turned to me, and with the same cutlet and the same wimpiness he reached to touch the side of my face. I didn't draw down. His cutlet touched me, ever so smoothly, and also he reached to draw me into the circle of his arms. I smelled his shirt, lately washed and sun- dried, and under it the clean manly scent of him.

We looked at each other, both of us silent, the whole room silent. And also Livia murmured and he smiled snappily and chucked me under the chin and left. I heard the screen door slam, and also the sounds of the auto as he drove to city. When I couldn't hear it presently I went over to the radio and switched it on. They were playing a Tammy Wynette song. " Stand by your man, " Tammy prompted, and my mama 's silence swallowed up the words.

While the radio played unheard I changed Livia and put her in for her nap. I came back to the kitchen and cleared the table. My mama gestured a hand at the air in front of her face.

"The smokes, " I said.

"I did n't say anything, " she said.

We did the dishes together. There's a dishwasher but we noway use it for the breakfast dishes. She prefers to run it only formerly a day, after the evening mess. It could hold all the day's dishes, they would not amount to further than one cargo in the machine, but she doesn't like to let the breakfast and lunch dishes stand. It seems extravagant to me, of time and trouble, and indeed of water, although our well furnishes further than we ever need. But it's her house, after all, and her dishwasher, and hers the decision as to when it's to be used.

Quietly she washed the dishes quietly I wiped them. As I reached to mound plates in a cupboard I caught her looking at me. Her eyes were on my impertinence, and I could feel her aspect right where I had felt Dan's cutlet. His touch had been light. Hers was firmer.

I said, " It's nothing. "

"All right. "

"Dammit, Mama! "

“I did n’t say anything, Tildie. ”

I was named Matilda for my father’s mama . I noway knew her, she failed before I was born, before my parents met. I was noway called Matilda. It was the name on my council parchment, on my motorist’s license, on Livia’s birth instrument, but no bone ever used it.

“He ca n’t help it, ” I said. “ It’s not his fault. ”

Her silence devoured my words. On the radio Tammy Wynette sang a song about divorce, spelling out the word. Why were they playing all her records this morning? Was it her birthday? Or an anniversary of some failed love?

“It’s not, ” I said. I moved to her right so that I could talk to her good observance.

“It’s a pattern. His father was vituperative to his mama . Dan grew up around that. His father drank and was free with his hands. Dan swore he'd noway be like that, but patterns like that are nearly insolvable to throw off. It’s what he knows, can you understand that? On a deep position, deeper than intellect, bone deep, that’s how he knows to bear as a man, as a hubby. ”

“He marked your face. He has n’t done that ahead, Tildie. ”

My hand flew to the spot. “ You knew that — ”

“Sounds trip. Indeed with my door unrestricted, indeed with my good observance on the pillow. I ’ve heard effects. ”

“You noway said anything. ”

“I did n’t say anything moment, ” she reminded me.

“He ca n’t help it, ” I said. “ You have to understand that. Did n’t you see him this morning?”

“I saw him. ”

“It hurts him further than it hurts me. And it’s my fault as much as it’s his. ”

“For allowing it? ”

“For provoking him. ”

She looked at me. Her eyes are a pale blue, like mine, and at times there's blameworthiness in them. My aspect must have the same quality. I've been told that it's piercing. “ Do n’t look at me like that, ” my hubby has said, raising a hand as much to shield off my aspect as to hang me. “ Damn you, do n’t you look at me like that! ”

Like what? I ’d wondered. How was I looking at him? What was I doing wrong?

“I do provoke him, ” I told her. “ I make him hit me. ”

“How? ”

“By saying the wrong thing. ”

“What kind of thing? ”

“Effects that upset him. ”

“And also he has to hit you, Tildie? Because of what you say? ”

“It’s a pattern, ” I said. “ It’s the way he grew up. Men who drink have sons who drink. Men who beat their women have sons who beat their women. It’s passed on over the generations like a inheritable illness. Mama, Dan’s a good man. You see how he's with Livia, how he loves her, how she loves him. ”

“Yes. ”

“And he loves me, Mama. Do n’t you suppose it tears him up when commodity like this happens? Do n’t you suppose it eats at him? ”

“It must. ”

"It does! " I allowed how he 'd cried last night, how he 'd held me and touched the mark on my impertinence and cried. "And we 're going to try to do commodity about it, " I said. " To break the pattern. There is a clinic in Fulton City where you can go for comforting. It's not precious, moreover. "

"And you 're going? "

"We 've talked about it. We 're considering it. "

She looked at me and I made myself meet her eyes. After a moment she looked down. " Well, you would know further about this kind of thing than I do, " she said. " You went to council, you studied, you learned effects. "

I studied art history. I can tell you about the Italian Renaissance, although I've formerly forgotten much of what I learned. I took one psychology course in my beginner time and we observed the geste of white rats in mazes.

"Mama, " I said, " I know you disapprove. "

"Oh, no, " she said. " Tildie, that's not so. "

"It's not? "

She shook her head. " I just hurt for you, " she said. " That's all. "

We live on 220 acres, only a third of them position. The ranch has been in our family since the land was cleared beforehand in the last century. It has been times since we tended it. The MacNaughtons run lamb in our north ranges, and Mr. Parkhill leases forty acres, planting alfalfa one time and field sludge the coming. Mama has some bank stock and some serviceability, and the tips plus what she's paid for the land rent are enough to keep her. There's no mortgage on the land and the levies have stayed low. And she has a big kitchen theater . We cat out of it all summer long and put up enough in the fall to carry us through the downtime.

Dan studied relative lit while I studied art history. He got a master's and did half the course work for a doctorate and also knew he could n't do it presently. He got a job driving a hack and I worked staying tables at Paddy Mac's, where we used to come for beer and hamburgers when we were scholars. When I got pregnant with Livia he did n't want me on my bases all day but we could n't make ends meet on his earnings as a cabdriver. Rents were high in that megacity, and everything bring a fortune.

And we both loved country living, and knew the megacity was no place to bring up Livia. So we moved then, and Dan got work right down with a construction company in Caldwell. That's the nearest city, just six long hauls from us on country roads, and Fulton City is only twenty- two long hauls.

After that discussion with Mama I went outdoors and walked back beyond the theater and the pear and apple estate. There's a sluice runs transversely across our land, and just beyond it's the spot I always liked the stylish, where the walnut trees are. We've a whole copse of black walnuts, twenty- six trees in all. I know because Dan counted them. He was trying to estimate what they 'd bring.

Walnut is precious. People will pay thousands of bones for a mature tree. They make veneer from it, because it's too expensive to use as solid wood.

"We ought to vend these off, " Dan said. " Your ma's got an untapped resource then. notoriety could come by, cut 'em down, and steal 'em. Like birders in Kenya, killing the mammoths for their ivory. "

"No bone's going to come onto our land. "

"You noway know. Anyway, it's a waste. You ca n't indeed see this spot from the house. And nothing does anything with the nuts. "

When I was a girl my ma and I used to gather the walnuts after they fell in early afterlife. Thousands fell from the trees. We'd just gather a basketful and crack them with a hammer and pick the meat out. My hands always got black from the cocoons and stayed that way for weeks.

We only did this a many times. It was after Daddy left, but while Grandma Yount was still alive. I do n't flash back Grandma bothering with the walnuts, but she did lots of other effects. When the cherries came in we'd all pick them and she'd singe pies and put up jars of the rest, and she 'd boil the recesses to clean them and suture scraps of cloth to make beanbags. There are still beanbags in the garret that Grandma Yount made. I 'd brought one down for Livia and fancied I could still smell cherries through the cloth.

" We could gather the walnuts, " I told Dan. " If you want. "

" What for? You ca n't get anything for them. Too important trouble to open and hardly any meat in them. I 'd sooner gather the trees. "

" Mama likes having them then. "

" They 're worth a fortune. And they 're a renewable resource. You could cut them and plant further and eventually they 'd put your grandchildren through council. "

" You do n't need to cut them to plant further. There's other land we could use. "

" No point planting further if you 're not going to cut these, is there? What do we need them for? "

" What do our grandchildren need council for? "

" What's that supposed to mean? "

" Nothing, " I 'd said, backing down.

And hours latterly he 'd taken it up again. " You meant I wasted my education, " he said. " That's what you meant by that crack, is n't it? "

" No. "

" also what did you mean? What do I need a master's for to hammer a nail? That's what you meant. "

" It's not, but putatively that's how you 'd rather hear it. "

He hit me for that. I guess I had it coming. I do n't know if I merited it, I do n't know if a woman deserves to get hit, but I guess I provoked it. commodity makes me say effects I should n't, effects he 'll take amiss. I do n't know why.

Except I do know why, and I 'd walked out of the kitchen and across to the walnut copse to keep from talking about it to Mama. Because he'd his pattern and I had mine.

His was what he 'd learned from his daddy, which was to abuse a woman, to poke her, to strike her with his fists. And mine was a pattern I 'd learned from my ma, which was to make a man leave you, to tease him with your mouth until one day he put his clothes in a wallet and walked out the door.

In the mornings it tore at me to hear the screen door slam. Because I allowed

, Tildie, one day you 'll hear that sound and it 'll be for the last time. One day you 'll do what your mama managed to do, and he 'll do like your father did and you 'll noway see him again. And Livia will grow up as you did, in a house with her mama and her grandmother, and she 'll have cherry- hole beanbags to play with and she 'll pick the meat out of black walnuts, but what will she do for a daddy? And what will you do for a man?

All the rest of that week he noway raised his hand to me. One night Mama stayed with Livia while Dan and I went to a movie in Fulton City. Subsequently we went to a place that reminded us both of Paddy Mac's, and we drank beer and got silly. Driving home, we rolled down the auto windows and sang songs at the top of our lungs. By the time we got home the beer had worn off but we were still happy and we hastened upstairs to our room.

Mama did n't say anything coming morning but I caught her looking at me and knew she 'd heard the old iron bedstead. I allowed

, You hear a lot, indeed with your good observance pressed against the pillow. Well, if she had to hear the fighting, let her hear the loving, too.

She could have heard the bed that night, too, although it was a quieter and gentler lovemaking than the night ahead. There were no knowing ganders the coming day, but after the screen door closed behind Dan and after Livia was in for her nap, there was a nice easiness between us as we stood side by side doing the breakfast dishes.

Subsequently she said, " I 'm so glad you 're back home, Tildie. "

" So you do n't have to do the dishes each by yourself. "

She smiled. " I knew you 'd be back, " she said.

" Did you? I wonder if I knew. I do n't suppose so. I allowed

I wanted to live in a megacity, or in a council city. I allowed

I wanted to be a professor's woman

and have humorless exchanges about literature and politics and art. I guess I was just a country girl each on. "

" You always loved it then, " she said. " Of course it'll be yours when I 'm gone, and I had it in mind that you 'd come back to it also. But I hoped you would n't stay that long. "

She had noway left. She and her mama lived then, and when she married my father he just moved by. It's a big old house, with different bodies added over the times. He moved by, and also he left, and she just stayed on.

I flashed back commodity. " I do n't know if I allowed

I 'd live then again, " I said, " but I always allowed

I would die then. " She looked at me, and I said, " Not so important bones then as be buried then. When we buried Grandma I allowed

, Well this is where they 'll bury me eventually. And I always allowed

that. "

Grandma Yount's grave is on our land, just to the east of the pear and apple estate. There are graves there dating back to when our people first lived then. The two children Mama lost are laid to rest there, and Grandma Yount's mama , and a great numerous children. It was n't that long ago that people would have four or five children to raise one. You ca n't read what's cut into utmost of the monuments, it's worn away with time, and it wears briskly now that we've the acid rain, but the monuments are there, the graves are there, and I always knew I 'd be there, too.

" Well, I 'll be there, too, " Mama said. " But not too soon, I hope. "

" No, not soon at each, " I said. " Let's live a long time. Let's be old ladies together. "

I allowed

it was a sweet discussion, a beautiful discussion. But when I told Dan about it we wound up fighting.

" When she goes, " he said, " that's when those walnuts go to request. "

" That's all you can suppose about, " I said. " Turning a beautiful copse into bones . "

" That timber's plutocrat in the bank, " he said, " except it's not in the bank because anybody could come by and haul it out of there behind our tails. "

" nothing's going to do that. "

" And other effects could be. It's no good for a tree to let it grow beyond its high. Insects can get it, or complaint. There's one tree formerly that was struck by lightning. "

" It did n't hurt it much. "

" When they 're my trees, " he said, " they 're coming down. "

" They wo n't be your trees. "

" What's that supposed to mean? "

" Mama's not leaving the place to you, Dan. "

" I allowed

what's mine is yours and what's yours is mine. "

" I love those trees, " I said. " I 'm not going to see them cut. " His face darkened, and a muscle worked in his jaw. This was a warning sign, and I knew it as similar, but I was stuck in a pattern, God help me, and I could n't leave it alone. " First you 'd vend off the timber, " I said, " and also you 'd vend off the realty. "

" I would n't do that. "

" Why? Your daddy did. "

Dan grew up on a ranch that came down through his father's father. unfit to make a living husbandry, first his forefather and also his father had vended off parcels of land little by little, whittling down at their effects and each time reducing the implicit income of what remained. After Dan's mama failed his father had stopped tilling altogether and drank full time, and the ranch was auctioned for aft levies while Dan was still in high academy.

I knew what it would do to him and yet I threw that in his face all the same. I could n't feel to help it, any further than he could help what followed.

At breakfast the coming day the silence made me want to scream. Dan read the paper while he ate, also hastened out the door without a word. I could n't hear the screen door when it banged shut or the auto machine when it started up. Mama's silence — and his, and mine — drowned out everything differently.

I allowed

I 'd burst when we were doing the dishes. She did n't say a word and neither didI. subsequently she turned to me and said, " I did n't go to council so I do n't know about patterns, or what you do and what it makes him do. "

The quattrocento and rats in a maze, that's all I learned in council. What I know about patterns and family violence I learned watching Oprah and Phil Donahue, and she watched the same programs I did.(" He bartered your eye and broke your nose. He demurred you in the stomach while you were pregnant. How can you stay with a brute like this? " " But I love him, Geraldo. And I know he loves me. ")

" I just know one thing, " she said. " It wo n't get better. And it'll get worse. "

" No. "

" Yes. And you know it, Tildie. "

" No. "

He had n't bartered my eye or broken my nose, but he'd pounded my face with his fists and it was swollen and discolored. He had n't demurred me in the stomach but he'd shoved me from him. I had been adhering to his arm. That was stupid, I knew better than to do that, it drove him crazy to have me hang on him like that. He'd shoved me and I 'd gone sprawling, wrenching my leg when I fell on it. My knee pained now, and the muscles in the front of that ham were sore. And my caricature pen was sore where he 'd punched me.

But I love him, Geraldo, Oprah, Phil. And I know he loves me.

That night he did n't come home.

I could n't sit still, could n't catch my breath. Livia caught my anxiety and would n't sleep, could n't sleep. I held her in my arms and paced the bottom in front of the TV set. Back and forth, back and forth.

At night eventually I put her in her crib and she slept. Mama was playing bijou at the pine table. Only the top is pine, the base is maple. An relic, Dan pronounced it when he first saw it, and better than the bones

in the shops. I suppose he'd it priced in his mind, along with the walnut trees.

I refocused out a move. Mama said, " I know about that. I just have n't decided whether I want to do it, that's all. " But she always says that. I do n't believe she saw it.

At bone

I heard our auto turn off the road and onto the clay. She heard it, too, and gathered up the cards and said she was tired now, she 'd just turn in. She was out of the room and up the stairs before he came in the door.

He was drunk. He lurched into the room, his shirt open halfway to his midriff, his eyes unfocused. He said, " Oh, Jesus, Tildie, what's passing to us? "

" Shhh, " I said. " You 'll wake the baby. "

" I 'm sorry, Tildie, " he said. " I 'm sorry, I 'm so goddam sorry. "

Going up the stairs, he spun down from me and staggered into the rail. It held. I got him upstairs and into our room, but he passed out the nanosecond he lay down on our bed. I got his shoes off, and his shirt and pants, and let him sleep in his socks and undergarments.

In the morning he was still sleeping when I got up to take care of Livia. Mama had his breakfast on the table, his coffee poured, the review at his place. He rushed through the kitchen without a word to anybody, tore out the door and was gone. I moved toward the door but Mama was in my path.

I cried, " Mama, he's leaving! He 'll noway be back! "

She glanced meaningfully at Livia. I stepped back, lowered my voice. " He's leaving, " I said, helpless. He'd started the auto, he was driving down. " I 'll noway see him again. "

" He 'll be back. "

" Just like my daddy, " I said. " Livvy, your father's gone, we 'll noway see him again. "

" Stop that, " Mama said. " You do n't know how important sticks in their minds. You mind what you say in front of her. "

" But it's true. "

" It's not, " she said. " You wo n't lose him that easy. He 'll be back. "

In the autumn I took Livia with me while I picked pole sap and summer squash. also we went back to the pear and apple estate and played in the shade. After a while I took her over to Grandma Yount's grave. We 'll all be then eventually, I wanted to say, your grandma and your daddy and your ma, too. And you 'll be then when your time comes. This is our land, this is where we all end up.

I might have said this, it would n't hurt for her to hear it, but for what Mama said. I guess it's true you do n't know what sticks in their minds, or what they 'll make of it.

She liked it out there, Livia did. She crawled right over to Grandma Yount's gravestone and ran her hand over it. You 'd have allowed

she was trying to read it that way, like a eyeless person with Braille.

He did n't come home for regale. It was going on ten when I heard the auto on the clay. Mama and I were watching TV. I got up and went into the kitchen to be there when he came by.

He was sober. He stood in the doorway and looked at me. Every emotion a man could have was there on his face.

" Look at you, " he said. " I did that to you. "

My face was worse than the day ahead. Bruises and bumps are like that, taking their time to grow.

" You missed regale, " I said, " but I saved some for you. I 'll heat up a plate for you. "

" I formerly ate. Tildie, I do n't know what to say. "

" You do n't have to say anything. "

" No, " he said. " That's not right. We've to talk. "

We slipped up to our room, leaving Mama to the TV set. With our door closed we talked about the patterns we were caught in and how we sounded to have no control, like actors in a play with all their lines written for them by someone differently. We could extemporize, we could construct movements and gestures, we could read our lines in any of a number of ways, but the script was all written down and we could n't get down from it.

I mentioned comforting. He said, " I called that place in Fulton City. I would n't tell them my name. Can you feature that? I called them for help but I was too shamed to tell them my name. "

" What did they say? "

" They would want to see us once a week as a couple, and each of us collectively formerly a week. Total price for the three sessions would be eighty bones

. "

" For how long? "

" I asked. They could n't say. They said it's not the kind of change you can anticipate to make overnight. "

I said, " Eighty bones

a week. We ca n't go that. "

" I had the feeling they might reduce it some. "

" Did you make an appointment? "

" No. I allowed

I 'd call hereafter. "

" I do n't want to cut the trees, " I said. He looked at me. " To pay for it. I do n't want to cut Mama's walnut trees. "

" Tildie, who brought up the damn trees? "

" We could vend the table, " I said.

" What are you talking about? "

“ In the kitchen. The pine- top table, did n’t you say it was an relic? We could vend that. ”

“ Why would I want to vend the table? ”

“ You want to vend those trees bad enough. You as much as said that as soon as my ma dies you ’ll be out back with a chain saw. ”

“ Do n’t start with me, ” he said. “ Do n’t you start with me, Tildie. ”

“ Or what? Or you ’ll hit me? Oh, God, Dan, what are we doing? Fighting over how to pay for the comforting to keep from fighting. Dan, what’s the matter with us? ”

I went to embrace him but he backed down from me. “ Honey, ” he said, “ we more be real careful with this. They were telling me about raising patterns of violence. I ’m hysterical of what could be. I ’m going to do what they said to do. ”

“ What’s that? ”

“ I want to pack some effects, ” he said. “ That’s what I came home to do. There’s that Drink Inn Motel outside of Caldwell, they say it’s not so bad and I believe they've daily rates. ”

“ No, ” I said. “ No. ”

“ They said it’s stylish. Especially if we ’re going to start comforting, because that brings everything up and out into the open, and it threatens the part of us that wants to be in this pattern. Tildie, from what they said it ’d be dangerous for us to be together right now. ”

“ You ca n’t leave, ” I said.

“ I would n’t be five long hauls down. I ’d be coming for regale some nights, we ’d be going to a movie now and also. It’s not like — ”

“ We ca n’t go it, ” I said. “ Dan, how can we go it? Eighty bones

a week for the comforting and Cod knows how important for the motel, and you ’d be having utmost of your refections out, and how can we go it? You ’ve got a decent job but you do n’t make that kind of plutocrat. ”

His eyes hardened but he breathed in and out, in and out, and said, “ Tildie, just talking like this is a strain, do n’t you see that? We can go it, we ’ll find a way to go it. Tildie, do n’t snare on to my arm like that, you know what it does to me. Tildie, stop it, will you for Cod’s sake stop it? ”

I put my arms around my own tone and hugged myself. I was shaking. My hands just wanted to take hold of his arm. What was so bad about holding on to your hubby’s arm? What was wrong with that?

“ Do n’t go, ” I said.

“ I've to. ”

“ Not now. It’s late, they wo n’t have any apartments left anyhow. stay until morning. Ca n’t you stay until morning? ”

“ I was just going to get some of my effects and go. ”

“ Co in the morning. Do n’t you want to see Livvy before you go? She’s your son, do n’t you want to say good- bye to her? ”

“ I ’m not leaving, Tildie. I ’m just staying a many long hauls from then so we ’ll have a chance to keep from destroying ourselves. My Cod, Tildie, I do n’t want to leave you. That’s the whole point, do n’t you see that? ”

“ Stay until morning, ” I said. “ Please? ”

“ And will we go through this again in the morning? ”

“ No, ” I said. “ I promise. ”

We were both restless, but also we made love and that settled him, and soon he was sleeping. I could n't sleep, however. I lay there for a time, and also I put a mask on and went down to the kitchen and sat there for a long time, thinking of patterns, thinking of ways to escape them. And also I went back up the stairs to the bedroom again.

I was in the kitchen the coming morning before Livia woke up. I was there when Mama came down, and her eyes widened at the sight of me. She started to say commodity but also I guess she saw commodity in my eyes and she stayed silent.

I said, " Mama, we've to call the police. You 'll mind the baby when they come for me. Will you do that? "

" Oh, Tildie, " she said.

I led her up the stairs again and into our bedroom. Dan lay downward , the way he always slept. I drew the distance down and showed her where I 'd picked him, slipping the kitchen cutter between two caricatures and into the heart. The cutter lay on the table beside the bed. I had wiped the blood from it. There hadn't been veritably important blood to wipe.

" He was going to leave, " I said, " and I could n't bear it. Mama. And I allowed

. Now he wo n't leave, now he 'll noway leave me. I allowed

. This is a way to break the pattern. Is n't that crazy. Mama? It does n't make any sense, does it? "

" My poor Tildie. "

" Do you want to know commodity? I feel safe now. Mama. He wo n't hit me presently and I noway have to worry about him leaving me. He ca n't leave me, can he? " commodity caught in my throat. " Oh, and he 'll noway hold me again, moreover. In the circle of his arms. "

I broke also, and it was Mama who held me, stroking my forepart, soothing me. I was each right also, and I stood up straight and told her she had better call the police.

" Livia 'll be up any nanosecond now, " she said. " I suppose she's awake, I suppose I heard her fussing a nanosecond agone

. Change her and bring her down and feed her her breakfast "

" And also? "

" And also put her in for her nap. "

After I put Livia back in her crib for her nap Mama told me that we were n't going to call the police. " Now that you 're back where you belong, " she said, " I 'm not about to see them take you down. Your baby needs her ma and I need you, too. "

" But Dan — "

" Bring the big oxcart around to the kitchen door. Between the two of us we can get him down the stairs. We 'll dig his grave in the reverse, we 'll bury him then on our land. People wo n't suspect anything. They 'll just suppose he went off, the way men do. "

" The way my daddy did, " I said.

Ever we got him down the stairs and out through the kitchen. The hardest part was getting him into the old oxcart. I checked Livia and made sure she was sleeping soundly, and also we took turns with the barrow, wheeling it out beyond the kitchen theater .

" What I keep allowing, " I said, " is at least I broke the pattern. "

She did n't say anything, and what she did n't say came one of her notorious silences, stinking up all the sound around us. The barrow's wheel grassed , the catcalls sang in the trees, but now I could n't hear any of that.

Suddenly she said, " Patterns. " also she did n't say anything further, and I tried to hear the squeak of the wheel.

Also she said, " He noway would have left you. If he left he 'd only come back again. And he noway would have quit hitting you. And each time would be a little worse than the last. "

" It's not always like it's on Oprah, Mama. "

" There's effects you do n't know, " she said.

" Like what? "

The grassing of the wheel, the song of catcalls. She said, " You know how I lost the hail in the one observance? "

" You had an infection. "

" That's what I always told you. It's not true. Your daddy cupped his hands and boxed my cognizance. He deafened me on the one side. I was lucky, nothing happed to the other observance. I still hear as good as ever out of it. "

" I do n't believe it, " I said.

" It's the verity, Tildie. "

" Daddy noway hit you. "

" Your daddy hit me all the time, " she said. " All the time. He used his hands, he used his bases. He used his belt. "

I felt a tightening in my throat. " I do n't flash back , " I said.

" You did n't know. You were little. What do you suppose Livia knows? What do you suppose she 'll flash back ? "

We walked on a ways. I said, " I just flash back the two of you holloing . I allowed

you cried and eventually he left. That's what I always allowed

. "

" That's what I let you suppose. It's what I wanted you to suppose. I had a broken jaw, I had broken caricatures, I had to keep telling the croaker

I was clumsy, I kept falling down. He believed me, too. I guess he'd lots of women told him the same thing. " We switched, and I took over the oxcart. She said, " Dan would have done the same to you, if you had n't done what you did. "

" He wanted to stop. "

" They ca n't stop, Tildie. No, not that way. To your left wing. "

" Are n't we going to bury him alongside Grandma Yount? "

" No, " she said. " That's too near the house. We 'll dig his grave across the sluice, where the walnut copse is. "

" It's beautiful there. "

" You always liked it. "

" So did Dan, " I said. I felt so funny, so light- headed. My world was turned upside down and yet it felt safe, it felt solid. I allowed

how Dan had itched to cut down those walnut trees. Now he 'd lie ever at their bases, and I could come back then whenever I wanted to feel close to him.

" But he 'll be lonely then, " I said. " Wo n't he? Mama, wo n't he? "

The walnut trees lose their leaves beforehand in the fall, and they put on lower of a color show than the other hardwoods. But I like to come to the copse indeed when the trees are bare. occasionally I bring Livia. More frequently I come by myself.

I always liked it then. I love our whole 220 acres, every square bottom of it, but this is my favorite place, among these trees. I like it indeed better than the graveyard over by the pear and apple estate. Where the graves have monuments, and where the women and children of our family are buried.

Chapter No. 9: The Winfield Trade

Venetia Scott said, " Slow down a bit and take this coming right. "

I looked over to her. " Much further? "

She shook her head. " Not further than a afar now. I really do appreciate your driving me from work,Mr. Cuddy. "

My new customer said it like she was thanking a server for bringing her an redundant blend hankie . About five- five andmid-thirties, Scott looked neat in a argentine herringbone suit with a ruffled white blouse and two- inch heels. Her face was thin, but she had big green eyes and generous lips and auburn hair drawn back into a bun that suggested at shoulder length formerly loosened.

Scott had called me at my office. A counsel who represented her bank in major loan deals had recommended me as a private investigator who could be trusted on a nonpublic matter. I told her I 'd call her back, also telephoned the counsel. Venetia Scott had checked out as a lately promotedvice-president in charge of computer parcel agreements for one of the many Boston fiscal institutions still taking aliment without government receivership. I 'd picked her up just fifteen twinkles ago outside one of the bank's branches, filling up the time more with small talk than business as she gave me directions to her home address.

"Ms. Scott, I take it whatever you want me to work on has to do with your house? "

" It does. "

" Just what, exactly? "

My customer took a deep breath. " Beginning about a month agone, someone has been staying there while I 've been down on weekends. "

It was Thursday as we were talking. " How do you know? "

" Little effects. And passions. I 'm veritably sensitive that way. "

Jesus. " Do you live alone? "

An icy tone. " What difference does that make? "

" What I mean is, could notoriety differently in the house be responsible? "

" No. Since my divorce, I live alone except for Winfield. "

" Winfield? "

" My cat. "

I smiled. " Named after Dave? "

" I supplicate your amnesty? "

" Dave Winfield. Yankee outfielder who was unhappy in New York, moved to a couple of other brigades since. "

The icy tone again. "Winfield isn't named after an athlete. He's named after Winfield Scott, a general in the Mexican- American War. I 'm a traceable assignee. "

" Oh. "

The cat turned out to be a tubby orange gib with unheroic eyes and long whiskers. He was tender enough, brushing against my pant bond and purring like a snoring lumberman when I scratched between his cognizance.

We were in the foyer of Scott's modest Cape Cod, the lowest house in a good neighborhood. A atrocious investment in themid-eighties, it was presumably holding its value as well as could be anticipated now. I 'd checked the frontal door on our way in. No sign of forced entry.

Scott walked me through a living room with social cabinetwork, including an old-fashioned slider president, to a kitchen extended via a sundeck into the vicinity. The aft door cinch and jamb looked OK , too.

" You keep your windows locked? "

" Always. "

" Security system? "

" No. "

I stepped out onto the sundeck and looked left, also right. Each skirting house was nestled on about an acre, hers only a half- acre by the aesthetics of the landscaping that acted as boundary lines.

" Neighbors? "

Scott refocused left. " That place has been empty for three months. Foreclosure, but not by my bank. " She swung right. " The couple on the other side have been in Florida for six weeks. Which is my point, really. "

" Your point? "

"Yes. However, there are better choices within easy reach, If someone simply wanted to break into a house and enthrall it like a squatter. No,Mr. Cuddy, this is importunity. "

" importunity. "

" Yes. Subtle, but clear. "

" Could you partake some of the craft with me? "

A labored shriek. " Toilet paper roll just slightly out of fettle. "

I looked down at Winfield, who had followed us from room to room. " perhaps the cat, toying with it? "

The icy tone a third time. " Water spectacles irrigated and dried, leaving no spots. Spoons placed in hole snags down rather than snags over. "

" Spoons. "

" I supplicate your — "

" Spoons plural, or just one each time "

" Just one. "

" Same for spectacles? "

" Yes. "

We moved back into the living room. " You suppose it's importunity, you must have notoriety in mind. "

" Three notabilities. Do you wish to take notes? "

I sat down in the slider president. Comfortable and silent.

Scott used her left hand to tick off names on her right, as though she were roundly polishing her nails. " First, Chris Murphy, myex-husband. He's a police officer in the coming city. "

Uh-oh. " He still have a set of keys to this place "

" No. The cinches have been changed doubly. "

" doubly? "

" Yes. formerly after the judge ordered him out during the divorce three times agone, and again five weeks agone. "

" Just before you noticed the ' subtle importunity. '"

" Exactly. That brings me to the alternate — what would you call it, 'questionable '? "

" The alternate person will do forfeiture. "

" Second is Luther Dane, my adjunct at the bank. I lost my keys at work, which was the reason I had the cinches changed again. Luther would have access to my new key. "

" This Dane have any motive? "

" Yes. He'd love to see me foul over due to pressure then so that he could get my job. "

" Is that realistic? "

" It's how I got my creation. "

" By forcing out a master? "

" Precisely. Which brings us to number three, Irene Presker. "

" Your former master. "

A nod. " I 'm sure she has it in for me after I nudged her out. "

I set up myself lodging for Presker but fought it. " She have access to your keys? "

" Not that I know of. "

" Who was the locksmith this last time "

A surge of the hand. " A nice man, got on famously with Winfield. Vietnamese, I suppose. He came by to change the cinches on a Friday just as I was leaving. "

" And the coming week, the live- in stuff began passing. "

" The coming weekend. "

" Why is it that you go down weekends, Ms. Scott? "

She glanced inevitably toward a shelf on the wall. I could see a framed print of Scott in casual clothes, hugging a handsome man of about fifty with argentine hair that looked precisely nominated indeed in the breath that lifted it.

My customer said, " I 'm seeing a man who's antipathetic to cat dander, so I spend weekends at his home. "

" Name? "

" I do n't want you approaching him. "

" I 'd just like his name in case it comes up. "

" Evan Speidel. "

I looked at the print again and took a conjecture. " Also in banking? "

" Yes. He 'll be the coming chairman of Ridgeview Savings and Loan, a solid institution. "

Scott put further into " solid " than I could have with a hammer.

" Speidel have a key to your house? "

The icy tone got glacial. " I keep a extra at his home. "

I glanced down at the cat. " Why not just give Winfield down? "

My customer glared at me. " I bought him for Chris firstly, but Winfield stayed with me as part of the divorce agreement. "

I masticated on that awhile.

Still, forget it, " If you 're allowing that Evan has anything to do with this. "

Actually, I was allowing that Venetia Scott might have been better off with the bobby that liked pussycats than the banker who could n't, but I kept it to myself.

On Friday morning I got up beforehand and went over the addresses Venetia Scott had given me. also I drove to the town area nearest her house.

The sign over the glass door said main road locksmith in drum- type. The walls of the six-by- seven shop were lined with brass clods and sturdy plates and assessing deadbolts. A skinny man with Southeast Asian features sat behind a sword counter with an English-language review open in front of him. His black hair hung over his forepart nearly to his eyebrows, and he worked a bony indicator cutlet one word at a time through a column that had the expression " Khmer Rouge " in its caption. Behind him, grandiloquent globules, threaded vertically on line, curtained entry to the reverse of the shop. The globules lustered a little as I closed the frontal door.

The man looked up at me, smiled and said, " Can I help, joe? "

I said, "Mr... "

" Hun is my name. "

I showed him my ID. He looked at it a long time, reading " John Francis Cuddy " as precisely as he'd the review.

" What you want? "

I pocketed the leather holder and explained that I was asking questions for Venetia Scott.

Hun's eyes grew cautious. "Ms. Scott? "

" Yes. "

" What's problem? "

" No problem for you. I 'd just like to ask you a many questions. "

Hun looked abnegated. " Ask. "

I refocused at the composition he 'd been reading. " You 're from Cambodia firstly? "

" Why that count? "

" No reason, except you 're reading an composition about the Khmer Rouge. "

Hun's jaw gripped. " I no need to read about Khmer Rouge. I live through Khmer Rouge. In Phnom Penh, also in camp, also in jungle. " He picked the paper with the tip of his cutlet. " review used to say two million people kill by Pol Pot. Now say only one million. How can this be? "

I did n't have an answer for him. " You changed the cinches atMs. Scott's house "

" Yes, I do that for her. "

" Anybody ever ask you for keys to the house? "

Hun's eyes widened. " Ask me? "

" Yes. "

" nothing. "

I went through the names I had, including the new swain, Evan Speidel. Hun shook his head no, the eyes stony at each one. I got the feeling that other interrogators had n't treated him so well in the history.

" Anyone differently then I could talk to? "

Hun's eyes went back down to the composition. " Is nothing differently. Only me. "

Chris Murphy, about six- two and two hundred pounds, looked like a cybersurfer who was losing his dishwater fair hair. And his temper at me.

" Cuddy, I do n't get why you 're asking me all these questions. "

" I 'm hired to ask questions. These are simple bones. "

" Simple, huh? Like am I draining myex-wife and you wo n't indeed tell me what I 'm supposed to be doing? "

I 'd called Murphy at police headquarters in the neighboring city, also awaited for him outdoors, as he 'd asked me to. We were standing next to a depressed, five- time-old Corvette that I took to be his auto. Murphy had his arms crossed, hefty hands working on the outside of his sport fleece.

" Murphy — "

" I mean, what the hell position am I in with the department, I get indicted of draining my partner, this day and age? "

" So you have n't been in any kind of contact with Venetia Scott. "

" No, I told you. Not her, not the bank, not the house. Not since the restraining order way back when. "

I had n't mentioned the house.

Murphy said, " You suppose I 'm nuts or commodity, a bobby violating a restraining order? "

I did n't suppose he was nuts. I did wonder how he and Venetia Scott ever got together, but I was n't sure I wanted to find out.

" Seen your cat recently? "

" My — Winfield? Hell, that little bugger still around? "

" How do you mean? "

" Aw, Venny, she noway watched important one way or the other for the cat. Just like another pawn in the chess game between her counsel and me. "

" Because you wanted him back? "

Murphy looked irritated. " Cuddy, she held onto him because I made her suppose I wanted him back. "

" Why would you do that? "

" So I could get what I wanted, like this auto, some other stuff to set myself up in a new place. "

" While she got the house. "

" Right, right. Hell, it was like a negotiating tactic on my part. What do you suppose, I 'm stupid? "

I let that one pass, too.

Irene Presker had answered her own telephone and now answered her own door. The condo complex was a nice one, low and by the ocean about eight long hauls south of Boston. From the parking lot, I 'd seen a little skyline through the gauze in the distance and a couple of sportful windjammers through the mist in the focus.

Presker, still, didn't look sportful herself. About five bases altitudinous, she was pushing a hundred fifty, substantially through the hips and shanks. Her hair was curled and too black to be natural, the make- up overdone considering she was supposedly working at home that day.

Gaping at my ID, Presker said, " Which would be easier for me, to talk with you or call the bobbies

? "

" Calling the bobbies, surely. "

The hint of a grin. " You 're really a private investigator? "

" Really and truly. "

"Each right, come in. "

The living room was a little box without fireplace or harbor view, a small, open kitchen cloistered with it. A corridor ran off in one direction toward two unrestricted doors, I assumed a bedroom and a bath. Presker took one barrel president, me the other, there not being space enough for settee or indeed loveseat.

" So, what's this about? "

" A former associate of yours is being wearied. Your name came up. "

" I 'm supposed to know commodity about ' a former associate ' being wearied? "

" That's what I 'm then to find out. "

" Hah. You wasted your gas. The only bone

I could... " Presker's eyes did grow sportful. " Not Venetia Scott? "

" Yes. "

" There's a God. I must thank Him. "

"Ms. Presker — "

" So, is Venny going nuts? "

Venny. The surname herex-husband had used. " You 're not indeed curious about what the importunity is "

" Not unless it's really awful. I 'd rather use my imagination. "

" Why so down on Scott? "

" Down. Down, now there's a great word for Venny. Put down, shut down, shot down. Lots of possibilities there. "

" Possibilities? "

" For who's draining her. Let me tell you commodity about your customer, Mr. Cuddy. Venny, principally speaking, is a witch. An absolute witch. She prayed me to take her on as my adjunct at the bank, and her résumé was n't in the labor force brochure before she was laying the root to replace me. Venny smelled up to people, slept with people, whatever it took. Oh, yeah, one other thing, too. She really did master the job. "

" Which is? "

" Doing loan papers on complicated computer plats. You know the slang? "

" None of it. "

" also I 'll spare you. Just figure that she can understand complicated connections, specialized and fiscal, also cover the bank as to them. "

" And you tutored her? "

" That's right. "

" And now she's in your office in a town hutment and you 're working out of your house. "

" Oh, but I 'm con- sult- ing. " A thick subcaste of affront carpeted Presker's voice. " My own home office. It's really much so much more meaningful and satisfying than a bare payment and stock options. "

It took me a nanosecond to appreciate that Presker was lampooning Scott's speech patterns.

" Anything you can tell me about who might be after her? "

Presker laughed, not a affable sound. " Try the joe who replaced her. perhaps he's literacy at the witch's knee. "

Luther Dane was a youthful black man with cornucopia- rimmed spectacles. I met him sitting at a office outside Venetia Scott's office in the hutment. He looked studious in a blue suit, white button- down shirt and quiet tie. At least until he started talking. also he both looked and sounded studious. “ I do n’t have any idea what could be behind this,Mr. Cuddy. ” Scott was at a meeting, so Dane and I had moved into her office, a nice view of the faceless and argentine field and a green harbor islet through a window that I was sure could n’t be opened. Dane had taken Scott’s office president without acting to suppose about it. I tried one of the captain’s chairpersons, my shoulders covering the hallmark of a original business academy blessed on the backrest.

“ No reason for anyone you know of to be drainingMs. Scott? ”

“ Venetia Scott is a warm and awful mortal being. ”

Dane’s words would have sounded fine to a bug planted in the office. His face and body language told a different story, like a Mideast hostage giving a mimetic TV interview.

“ You ’re not interested in spooking her out of her job? ”

“Ms.V. Scott doesn't scarify. ”

“ Rattle her also. Enough so she starts to make miscalculations then at work. ”

“ Her miscalculations would be looked upon as my miscalculations, too. ”

“ Not if you created the record rightly. ”

Dane smiled. “ Law academy, —Mr. Cuddy? ”

“ A time, nights. You? ”

“ Four times, nights. Worked long and hard to get this far. I ’m not about to contaminate my own well. ”

“ So, if you ’re not interested in spooking or rattling your master, how do you plan to get ahead? ”

“ By outworking her. Her and anybody differently I ’m contending with. ”

“ And you figure you can outworkMs. Scott. ”

“ The way she’s spending her weekends? You go. ”

I had n’t said anything about weekends. “ How’s that? ”

“ Her weekends, man. She’s spending them nearly differently. ”

“ How do you know? ”

Dane spread his hands wide, encompassing Scott’s office. “ Because I come in every Saturday and half a day on Sunday,Mr. Cuddy. I ’m then, and she is n’t, and that means she’s off nearly. ”

“ Like at her house? ”

“ Not when I try to reach her there. ”

“ Why would you try to do that? ”

Dane signed. “ Indeed on weekends, questions come up that I ’m not good enough to answer. ”

“ Yet. ”

Just a smile.

After speaking with Luther Dane, I did n’t stay for Venetia Scott to come back from her meeting. rather I got my auto out of hock at the parking garage next to the bank and drove to the suburban city where Ridgeview Savings and Loan had its services.

I sat outside the red- bricked and golden- domed structure for an hour before being awarded by the appearance of Evan Speidel. He shook two sets of hands on his way from the main entrance to a black Lincoln Continental. Inside the Lincoln, Speidel drove sedately about three long hauls to a botcher block and ferns taproom just off a busy boardwalk. I situated three slanting rows down from his auto and followed him into the eatery.

When he shook a many further hands and took a table, I slid onto a coprolite at the bar, the glass above the top shelf bottles allowing me to watch Speidel in reflection. After a server presented him with a Wall Street Journal to skim, a blend waitress brought him what looked like a dry manhattan without his having to order it. He glanced up a couple of times, like a man watching for someone to join him.

Someone did.

Irene Presker rushed through the place, still made up but now dressed like Venetia Scott had been in bankers ' tweeds. Speidel took one of Presker's hands in both of his as greeting. also they sat down across from each other and began talking. I could n't see any way of getting out of there without her spotting me, so I sat still and nursed a beer.

They talked through a drink and lunch and were about to order cate when Presker caught me out of the corner of her eye. She slightly broke, covering it with a win- up gesture to support her chins. signaling off coffee, the adviser awaited until Speidel covered the tab by subscribing for it, also shook hands farewell with him as he moved toward the exit and she toward the rest apartments.

Presker made sure Speidel was gone ahead reversing direction and storming up to the bar. " What's the idea of following me? "

" perhaps I did n't believe everything I heard at your condo. "

" Does that mean you have to give me a heart attack in the middle of an interview? "

" Interview "

" The man who just left is "

Presker stopped, but I had n't intruded her.

I said, " Who's he? "

She tapped a stocky cutlet on my left arm. " He left before I did, but he was then before I was. I would have noticed you taking this coprolite if you came in after me. That means you were then before me. " Presker looked sportful again. " And that means that either you 've tapped my phone, in which case you would n't have bothered covering this little meeting, or you 're following my lunch date. But why? "

I got up before telling Presker anything differently, feeling my customer might be a little disappointed in me.

I sat in my auto until Irene Presker came out. She noticed me, as I 'd hoped she would, but just blew me a kiss, which meant I was n't chaffing her at all.

I started up and drove back toward the megacity, allowing as stylish I could. Chris Murphy might have bullied Hun the locksmith into giving him the new key to Venetia Scott's house. Murphy also could have used a shell master from his department, but where was his motive three times after the divorce? Luther Dane could have lifted the new key eventually at work, had it copied, and returned it before Scott realized it was missing, but he really did n't feel to suppose he demanded to reduce his master to displant her. Irene Presker might have gotten the spare key to the house from Evan Speidel, in which case her barranca at the bar was one for the record books. Speidel might be suitable to slip down from Scott on one of their weekends at his place, but why go to her place to do, basically, nothing?

Shaking my head, I concentrated on the business. At least I knew where that was going.

Luther Dane's voice said, "Ms. Scott's office. "

I said, " May I speak with her? "

" I 'll see, Mr. Cuddy. "

Good at feting voices, Mr. Dane.

" Venetia Scott. "

" Can Dane hear us? "

" No. "

" You 're positive? "

" Yes. What's it? "

" Given that it's Friday, are you going to Speidel's place "

" Yes. Why? "

" I've an idea. "

It was commodity I 'd hoped I could avoid. Solo, you ca n't really watch a house fully from the road or the reverse or the sides. Short of a high perch, there are just too numerous eyeless spots created by the structure itself. But, proprietor willing, you can cover it enough completely from one place.

Inside it.

In the dark, I sat on the slider in the living room, Winfield coiled up on my stage. I 'd paced off the strides to both frontal and aft doors. The slider was nearly exactly equidistant from each.

It was slightly eight o'clock when I heard commodity at the aft door. Winfield jumped off my stage and did his rotund stylish to gallop out there. I moved to the wall by the kitchen, hoping I was n't going to need a armament. I heard the faint sound of the door opening, also closing, also nothing.

I awaited five seconds. also ten. At fifteen, I went into the kitchen.

Nothing. Not indeed Winfield.

I looked out the windows, but did n't see anything. I went back to the living room and sank into the slider. I allowed about it, also allowed some further. About what I 'd told people, and what I had n't told them.

Ultimately, I believed I saw it.

I knocked on the door to themini-mansion a alternate time. Evan Speidel opened it. He was wearing a silk mask that presumably bring further than my rent. " Yes? " Nice baritone voice, too. " I need to speak with Venetia Scott. "

" At this hour? "

" Tell her it's John Cuddy. "

The door closed in my face. Two twinkles latterly, Scott restarted it.

Her mask matched Speidel's, her auburn hair indeed tumbling onto her shoulders. " This had better be important. "

I stepped inside the house. " It wo n't take long. There's bad news and good news. "

" What's the bad news? "

" I suppose we 've lost Winfield. "

I heard Speidel chuckle from the other room, but Scott's face stayed neutral. " That I can live with, I guess. What's the good news? "

Still, I can end it tonight, nothing getting hurt or in trouble, " If you 'll trust me to guarantee that it's over. "

The superintendent in Scott strengthened. " Guaranteed? "

"Absolutely. But I keep everything I 've learned to myself. "

My customer took ten seconds to weigh that. “ Do it. ”

This time I kept knocking until a shadow impended in the weak light behind the grandiloquent globules. Hun’s head gazed out, shook, also came forward sluggishly with the rest of his body as he let me into the shop.

I said, “ Where’s the cat? ”

He allowed about toughing it out, also said, “ In the reverse. Where I live. ”

“ Tied up? ”

Hun gave me a pathetic look and wrangle out a word I did n’t understand. Winfield came running, braked only a little by the blob curtain, utmost of which he could get under. He regarded me but snuggled up to Hun.

The locksmith said, “ How you know it was me? ”

“The other people I talked to, the other names I asked you about, I did n’t tell any of them the problem had commodity to do with Ms. Scott’s house. ”

Hun shook his head. “ That isn't enough. ”

“ No, but Scott said you really liked the cat. And at her house only the lowest effects were disturbed, like someone was visiting, not bogarting. ”

I stopped, but Hun jounced.

I said, “ Only the effects you would need to give him food and yourself water and relief. ”

“ I like to give him food. I like to visit him. ”

“ And grounded on what I told you, you might miss the chance to see him again. ”

“ You tell me problem with house, perhaps problem with cinches. perhapsMs. Scott not use me coming time to change cinches. perhaps I can not see Winfield again without break in. ”

“ Which you did n’t want to do. ”

“ I'm locksmith! I don't break in houses! ”

“ But you ’d risk your business to see the cat. ”

Hun reached down to stroke Winfield’s head. “ I lose my whole family, Khmer Rouge. This cat only critter all United States nice to me. ”

“ So you were willing to trade your profession for being suitable to have him. ”

The stony look. “ Yes. ”

“ Ever hear of Dave Winfield? ”

“ Who? ”

“ Skip it. ”

Chapter No. 10: A Hotel in Bucharest

The lift in the Harmonia had sounded slightly questionable when he'd arrived the evening before, but Gerald risked it. He got to the first bottom without mishap, and in the breakfast room he set up a long table spread with cold flesh and fish, two kinds of rolls and plenitude of chuck, several different logjams, and a toaster oven. It wasn't unlike the breakfast handed in any Scandinavian hostel. Gerald got a plateful of this and that, poured himself a mug of thick, black coffee, and settled down at a table.

" Is your woman not feeling up to breakfast "

The question, startling him out of his studies, came from a woman at the table to his right. She had soft, brown hair, gestured in a rather old- fashioned style, and a sympathetic smile. The man facing her across the table watched in a detached manner, as if he was used to her approaching nonnatives.

" I 'm hysterical I do n't actually have a woman. I 'm a companion. "

" Oh — I'm sorry. I do apologize. Robbie said there was another couple arriving history evening, and I allowed... Well, Tarom do their stylish, but they ever do n't manage to make people feel confident. And the field is just a bit scary after dark. "

" I 'd clearly agree about that... You said another couple? "

" Wanting to borrow one of the orphans. We always call them that, though utmost of them are abandoned, poor little diminutives. "

Light had actualized on Gerald. He'd anticipated, having chosen a middle- priced hostel, that some of the guests there would be on that sad hunt.

" Are there a lot of people then looking for a child to borrow? "

" Oh yes — relatively a lot. All ethnicities — French, German, Scandinavian. But the Harmonia prides itself on its British connections, going back to before the war. There are other feathers of British guests then too intelligencers, businessmen, sightseer people... "

" Ah, I 'm a sightseer person, " said Gerald, spreading a alternate roll with the rich, sweet jam that he'd set up veritably palatable. " And a intelligencer too. I 'm going to do a series of papers for the Yorkshire Post on Romania — I live near York, by the way. What I 'm really then for, however, is to skewer around hospices and sightseer venues. I 'm thinking of starting up a specialist trip establishment. Everyone who's been then since the revolution says the sightseer eventuality is immense. "

" Peasants, " said the man suddenly. " The Balkans are the last place in Europe where you can find peasants. "

He was in his late forties, wearing an anonymous suit and a council tie Gerald couldn't place. But the air of detachment, indeed of being nothing- veritably- much, was belied by sharp, living eyes.

" I do n't suppose the Romanian government would be happy if we pushed the ' peasant ' line too far, " Gerald explained. " Though the folk element could come into it — in fact it always does in package tenures. For some reason it makes people feel better about mass tourism. "

“ Well, it’s nice to have met you, ” said the woman, standing up. “ We must get on to another day of being passed from pillar to post. I ’m Eileen Kershaw, by the way, and this is my hubby Roland. ”

“ How do you do. I ’m Gerald Coutts. ”

Still, come up to the bar, “ If you ’re not doing anything tonight. We generally meet in the bar, to bandy progress, or lack of it. The Panorama Bar’s on the top bottom, and Radu the barman is veritably sweet, and knows us all. ”

Still, ” Gerald promised, “ If I do n’t have anything on I ’ll come up.

When he'd finished the last drop of a alternate mug of coffee Gerald went back to the foyer and decided not to risk the lift back to the third bottom. He still considered himself a youthful man forty- two, and veritably little sign of running to fat. Gradationally, however, as he trudged up the dimly lit stairwell, he came gripped by a feeling that he'd known he was going to get at some time or other in Romania the feeling of being watched. It persisted when he pushed the door through to the inversely murky corridor on the third bottom one imagined Securitate men in apartments noting appearances and goings, clocking up meetings in the corridors, playing through chivied exchanges of hostel guests — everything managed, manipulated, as if the guests were forced to dance some ludicrous minuet to music from a manic party headquarters.

A door opened at the far end of the corridor. A youthful couple surfaced, talking and laughing — she golden, healthy, and altitudinous, with a Valkyrie figure, he scourged, athletic, and handsome. The perfect Siegmund and Sieglinde, similar as you can only conceive in your mind’s eye, noway see on the melodramatic stage. As they passed him Gerald heard the man say “ I ’ve had worse at the Majestic in Tunbridge Wells, ” and their horselaugh echoed in the stairwell.

He shook off his feeling of oppression, of minatory watchers. effects had changed this was now a world of normal people, a part of the new Europe.

His morning was spent with Ministry people and with people lower down in the sightseer business. Everyone tried to be collaborative, though Gerald felt this was commodity new for them and they did n’t really know how. The rainfall was noble for October, and he ate lunch outdoors at the Athenee Palace. When he got back at late evening to the Harmonia he collected his passport from event along with his key.

“ I ’m sorry, we still ’ adieu to check — just like the old days. ”

The clerk who handed it over was a broad, rotund man with a gleeful smile that sounded to hide a natural melancholy.

“ Do n’t mention it. hospices in utmost European countries check passports. ”

“ Really? We don't know, you see. ”

“ Dare I risk the lift up to the Panorama Bar? ”

“’ E’s been mended moment. Use ’ im while ’ e is ’ ealthy ”

The lift opened straight out into the bar, which had a splendid view over the uncertain lights of Bucharest, and which was ringing with horselaugh and discussion. The presiding genius was Radu, the roly- poly barman, who sounded to set the relaxed tone of the place. English couples were mixing and switching gests with couples of other ethnicities, and the single people — doubtless the businessmen and intelligencers the Kershaws had mentioned — formed their own little groups. Eileen and Roland Kershaw hailed him, and he went over to talk to them. They were round a table with the Wagnerian couple he'd passed in the corridor.

" We saw our baby moment! " said Eileen triumphantly. " I held her! "

" Has she got a name? "

" Elena. It's a lovely name, is n't it? We 're not going to change it to Helen. We want her to know she's Romanian. We 'll bring her back then when she's aged, so she always feels at home. Oh — this is Ursula Upjohn and Edward Upjohn. "

" Ed, " said the Siegmund youthful man. He did n't feel like an Ed. They both were so youthful and vital and healthy that it was odd to suppose of them as unfit to have children — and delicate to suppose of a reason why they should n't borrow. maybe they wanted a baby — there were veritably many of those available for relinquishment in Britain, Gerald knew. Anyway, it hardly sounded polite to ask.

" How are effects going with you? " he asked Ursula.

" Oh, we 're at about the same stage as Eileen and Roland. We hope — fritters crossed — to be suitable to take Mihai home coming visit. "

" I suppose effects are noway certain, noway clear- cut. "

" noway, ever, " said Ed feelingly.

" That's why we 're so lucky to have Robbie, " said Ursula. " He'sfantastic.However, or a way of cutting through red tape recording, Robbie will find it, If there's a way of getting round problems. "

" There he's now, " said Roland. " That must be the new couple. "

When Robbie had surfaced from the lift, half the heads in the room had turned in his direction — some with a kind of starved stopgap in their eyes, rather as those with a need for faith will feast on some cut- price messiah. But there was nothing shifty or bargain-basement about Robbie. He was a clean- cut man in hismid-forties, in a smart, claret-colored blazer, carrying five or six lines. He'd smiles all round, but he made originally for a couple sitting a little away from the rest, not yet completely integrated. The man was cherubic, nearly boyish, with fair curled hair and a wicked smile. clearly he could be no further than thirty. His woman was a woman of forty-odd, hair cut short and starting to go argentine, dressed in a oppressively cut suit. commodity superintendent in original government, Gerald guessed.

" That's Laura Perceval, " said Ursula. " And Terry. They were out at the Ploesti orphanage this autumn "

" You should have brought them over and introduced them, " said Eileen. " You 're not doing your duty. "

" Yes, I should. They sounded awfully nice. From Derbyshire, I suppose. "

Tactfully nothing mentioned the distinction in their periods. No prizes for guessing why they could n't borrow in Britain, Gerald allowed. Robbie was questioning them — first one, also the other, turning his face to look into theirs, the couple leaning forward, interested, concerned, questioning in their turn.

" Robbie always takes new couples to the Ministry on their first morning, " said Ed. " They 're used to people from Romchild — that's our association. also he leaves them on their own — with a little distance of suggested way. It's a kind of throwing- in at the deep end. "

" We 've seen one! We 've set up one, we suppose! "

The cry was from another new couple, and was the signal for congratulations, backslappings, toasts. The groupings were breaking up, and Gerald took advantage of the interruption to slip down. The new couple was a thick- set, rubicund Yorkshire businessman, Mike Lawson, with a strong but affable accentuation, and his woman Mareeka, a beautiful Indian woman, wearing a sari, with a sophisticated Southern accentuation and measureless charm.

" He's a champion little fellow, " Gerald heard Mike say, beaming happily.

" Well, you 've really got reason to wear your sari tonight, " Eileen said to Mareeka. So she did n't always, Gerald allowed she was in that intriguing outback between East and West. outlands were always fascinating. Come to that,post-Ceausescu's Romania was one. Gerald introduced himself to one of the intelligencers and was soon drooling to him and a London businesswoman who joined them about motifs of common interest. But he was fascinated by the couples and kept his eye on them all evening, watching Robbie go from one couple to another — interested, encouraging, concerned — and eventually end up the center of an adoring, immensely gleeful group. He was, it sounded, a source of stopgap, a lamp of light.

In the coming many days Gerald sounded to get busier and busier, and was soon taking off from Bucharest in a hired auto, consecrating possible routes and pretensions for unborn passages. There was, as he'd anticipated, immense sightseer eventuality, combined with coming to no knowledge of the imperatives of mass tourism. There were possibilities far and wide he went that kept him constantly agitated. But he generally set up himself back at the Harmonia in the evening and enjoying a drink in the Panorama Bar. Then he could follow the progress and bummers of the colorful couples, and respect the way Robbie would go around raising spirits and suggesting ways round or through the roadblocks that officialdom erected.

" You do a awful job, " he said to him one evening.

" I 'm a Northerner, " said Robbie. " In Pontefract we do n't take no for an answer. "

" How frequently does it take a fix to change a ' no ' to ' yes '? "

Robbie winked.

" It's the last resort. Officially it's against Romchild's principles. We do n't like doing it because if we did it too readily we 'd be doing it all the time. But now and also... "

Gerald spoke to the newest couple one morning over breakfast. Laura and Terry Perceval, he'd noticed, were always veritably purposeful, eating and drinking while they were planning their day and their coming moves, and making notes in a little blackbook.However, he did n't feel to bear like one, If Terry had the aesthetics of a toyboy.

" The trouble with social services people in Britain, " said Laura hastily, after they had gabbled for a bit and got round to the ineluctable content, " is that they ca n't see beyond their tips. And because of the press they 're spooked corpus of making the fewest mistake. They do n't want to know about anything outside their own little boundaries. You tell them that the situation for orphans then's hopeless and they mime. "

" And believe me, it's hopeless, " said Terry. " We 've only scraped the face, but we know. "

" Because they 're so spooked of the press they try to live in an ideal world, " Laura went on. " Model two- parent families, him aged than her, he in a job, she at home, black parents for black children... "

" Life is a lot messier than that, " said Terry. " There are different feathers of connections. And people with no connections who would make excellent parents. "

" But you have to have some kind of instrument of fitness to take your baby into Britain when the time comes, do n't you? " Gerald asked.

" Oh yes, " said Terry. " generally. "

" We've ours, " said Laura forcefully.

" I suppose you suffered a lot of prying to get it? "

" Sheer bloody impertinence, " she replied, her mouth set in a grim line.

Utmost of the couples sounded to spend two or three weeks at a time in Romania, also return home and consolidate their position by postal or telephone connections(though the ultimate were veritably delicate). The more educated bones like Eileen and Roland Kershaw obviously had a whole lot of other couples in England to communicate , compare notes with, support. While they were in Romania much of the couples ' time was spent staying, or was just filled up in some way or other. Gerald went to a musicale at the Atheneum and in the interval, when it was the done thing to boardwalk around the entrance hall under the great pate, Gerald met up with Mike Lawson and Edward Upjohn.

" Mareeka would n't come, " said Mike, in his broad Yorkshire accentuation. " Says that every movement in Mahler's too long by ten twinkles. "

" She 'd be well advised not to say that anywhere near the Festival Hall, " said Gerald. " She might get lynched. "

" Ursula's a medieval music freak, " said Ed. " And I 'm a philistine. I jog to Nigel Kennedy pops on my particular stereo, and lift weights to the stylish of James Last. I came on because there was a spare ticket. "

" I suppose of you as a rather Wagnerian couple, " said Gerald. " Fighting dragons and defending holy grails. "

" Sorry to fail you. A propos, do you want to walk back with us? The thoroughfares are so dark, and there 've been a lot of thefts. "

" Really? I 've felt impeccably safe. But I 'd be happy to walk back with you. "

When they got back to the Harmonia they set up Robbie poring over passports and papers with the friendly receptionist, both veritably serious as befitted people engaged in satisfying the fiats of bureaucracy. Robbie gestured.

" See you in the Panorama, " he cried.

" You missed Mahler's Sixth, " said Gerald to Mareeka in the bar, where she was belting a brandy. " It was veritably good. "

" I 'm rather like Ursula, " said Mareeka coolly. " Anything latterly than Haydn is a bit suspect. Beethoven was a big mistake, and indeed Mozart occasionally went too far. "

The coming day Gerald directed his auto up to Sinaia. Everyone had told him it was one of the ineluctable pretensions of any package stint he might put together, and they were right. The summer palace of the Hohenzollern lords was the copywriter's dream a series of structures in majestic- feudal style, set in the mountain's side, the innards darkly rustic but grandiose the headquarters of Heme the Hunter. The place was, Gerald noted, relatively innocent of the requirements of tourism there wasn't a card in sight, nor a guidebook, and supervision was minimum. He felt both wonder and some qualm at the changes tenures like the bones he was planning would bring.

As he came out blinking into the sun and headed toward the lodge which had served as a pens ' retreat for the hymners of Ceausescu's greatness, Gerald suddenly broke in his stride that feeling had come upon him again, that feeling of being watched. Eerie. He shook himself presumably it was some kind of transference from the old days, for the pens when they were over then must have had a close eye kept on them for any sign of falling from a posture of total devotion to the Great Conductor.

The feeling faded as soon as it came. He saw Eileen Kershaw approaching from the lodge and signaling .

" Hello! You noway said you were coming up then. "

" Oh, I 'm going each over. "

" Mareeka's around nearly. She has n't seen it. This is my alternate visit. Is n't it awful? "

" Absolutely awful. "

" And just staying for package excursionists. "

Gerald smiled wryly.

" You make it sound rather dreadful. I 'm hoping to have small, differencing groups. "

" I 'm sure you are. And it'll do so much good to the frugality. But it wo n't be quite the same, will it? "

" Not relatively. But Romania has been so cut off. The further connections it has with the rest of Europe, the better. "

" That's right, " said Mareeka, who had just rambled over from the direction of the palace. " We need to get people interested in the place. They were at the time of the revolution, but also it sort of tagged off. People's attention span seems to get shorter and shorter. But the Romanians are so anxious to learn how effects are done in the West. "

" That's not absolutely an undiluted blessing, " said Eileen. " notoriety had her handbag snared back near the eatery an hour agone. Just like Florence or Rome. They say effects like that hardly ever happed before the revolution. "

" Under Ceausescu nothing had anything worth stealing, " said Gerald. " I still feel a lot safer then in Romania than I would on the thoroughfares of London or Edinburgh. "

But the content of crime pursued him during his remaining days in Romania — tales of thefts in the nearly black thoroughfares of darkness Bucharest, tales of the illegal plutocrat-changers turning nasty and demanding Western currency with imminences, rumors that the miners were poised to come back to the capital, with stories of what they had done the last time they took over the thoroughfares there. The couples were getting more uneasy, or maybe using the stories to justify themselves in taking children from that terrain. Gerald saw no substantiation himself of any rising drift of crime, and rather mocked all their stories. also, two days before he was due to return home, he heard that the receptionist at the Harmonia, the man he'd spoken to on his alternate day, had been knifed on his way home and killed.

" It's not as though he was likely to be carrying the takings home with him, " said Mike Lawson. " It's just horrible and senseless. "

For Gerald, however, the trip had gone well. Officialdom, sluggishly and uncertainly, had opened up under his patient negotiating ways arrangements had been come to, pledges made, planners listed. The more he'd seen of the country, the further awful it sounded. Whatever bone's dubieties about mass tourism, it had to be a good thing to open up similar beauty and interest to sympathetic trippers.

For some of the couples, too, effects were going well. Roland and Eileen, as they had hoped, were indurate in on their prospects of espousing Elena. They had been assured that their coming trip would be their last, and they could also take her home with them. Terry and Laura Perceval — maybe backed by Laura's experience in government, which was in fact at public position rather than the original position which Gerald had guessed at — had a definite prospect of relinquishment on their first trip, commodity of a record. They showed round photos in the Panorama Bar of Laura holding the bitsy baby girl at the door of the orphanage, with Terry leaning over her shoulder and tweaking the laughing baby's nose. It all sounded so good, so salutary, so normal. Gerald left with numerous good wishes and some pledges that at some time in the future numerous of them, with their children, would come on one of his tenures.

In the months that followed, Gerald went several times to Romania, but he noway spent further than one night at the Harmonia. He was probing Cluj, Timisoara, Constanta, and he always flew on to one or other of the municipalities coming day, after the ritual meetings with Ministry or tourism officers. On one of his late stays he set up Laura and Terry Perceval at the Harmonia, and heard that effects were progressing well with their relinquishment. On another occasion he set up Robbie there, but he was so busy with the affairs of new couples whom he was helping over the delicate first hurdles that Gerald did n't manage to do further than change a many words of chatting with him. On his last visit before the first of the tenures was listed to take place, he set up Mike Lawson behind him in the field line to take the aeroplane home.

" Great to see you again. Where's Mareeka? " he asked.

" She did n't come this time. This was just a quick ' sorting- out ' visit, to see some Ministry troublemakers. "

" Successful? "

" veritably. The coming trip is going to be the one. "

When he 'd gone through the formalities Gerald awaited for Mike as he checked his luggage through, but Mike decided to go Smoking.

" Did n't realize you did, " said Gerald.

" We Yorkshiremen have all the vices, and damn the intermeddlers who want to make us live healthily and ever. Actually, it's the strain of this business. I was down to one or two a day, but I 'm well over again now. "

It was after his first stint had taken place, and been a noble success, that Gerald set up a brief pause in his life. The content of the Romanian " orphans, " though no longer hot news, was noway entirely out of it obstructive original authorities in Britain who regarded the abdications with disapprobation; a couple who had set up " cling " insolvable with their espoused child; a couple who had smuggled their baby in. The intelligencer in Gerald had been dormant for a time, and it now reasserted itself. How had the couples that he'd come to know so well fared with their espoused children? There was clearly a story there, perhaps three or four.

It was just a question of getting in touch, because there had been no exchange of addresses. Robbie, he knew, came from Pontefract, but as his surname was Taylor tracking him down might be delicate. He sounded to flash back the Percevals came from Derbyshire, but he was n't sure which city. The Kershaws he allowed came from Luton (how awful — to borrow a child and bring it up in Luton!), and the Upjohns from London nearly. Mike

Lawson's luggage he'd seen at the field in Bucharest. He couldn't flash back the address, but it had been Huddersfield, and he knew Mike was in the carpet business. It was with Mike, obviously, that he should make a launch. When he drove to Huddersfield a couple of days latterly he set up the establishment in the Yellow runners, but when he chimed he was told that Mike was down on a buying trip to London.

"Stupid of me. I should have pealed in advance. Do you suppose you could give me his home number "

The reason he hadn't tried to communicate Mike and Mareeka in advance was his intelligencer's instinct that the truest picture comes from a surprise visit no time to prepare a false print. He knew from all those press reports that some of the abdications had been deliriously successful, others less so. He compared the number with the fourM. Lawsons in the telephone book and drove out to the address. There was a good chance, he felt, that Mareeka, with the new baby, would be at home.

The house was a substantial gravestone one, presumably late-puritanical, with a small frontal theater onto the road, land stretching out to the reverse, and a row of semis forming the rest of the road. Not at all a bad place in which to bring up a child. Gerald was disappointed, however, to get no response to his ring on the doorbell.

" They 're both out, " came a cry from coming door. An senior man, wrinkled and rainfall-beaten, was trimming his barricade in the nearest of the semis. " I suppose Mike is in London for a many days. "

Gerald went over.

" Yes, they told me he was down on business at the shop. I allowed his woman might be in. "

The man stopped trimming.

" His woman? Mr. Lawson does n't have a woman. "

" But Mareeka... Oh, maybe they 're not married. "

" Who? noway heard of a name like that. Mr. Lawson's noway been married, and there's no woman has lived then since his mama failed. Oh — it would n't be youthful Edward's woman you 'd be looking for, would it? "

" Edward? "

" His whoreson Ed. He's been living with Mike for a bit. He's disassociated from his woman, Mike says, and he's just got guardianship of their child. He's home utmost of the day since the little boy came, but he's shopping in Leeds moment. Was it his woman you were looking for? She's noway lived then, to my knowledge. "

" No, it... it was n't her. I suppose I 've made a mistake. "

On the way home Gerald stopped at a cantina on the outskirts of the city, bought lunch and a pint, and tried to suppose effects through. What he'd seen in Bucharest had been an elaborate façade and facade . Robbie Taylor was running an association to help people well-heeled people, no mistrustfulness who had no chance, or coming to none, of espousing in Britain. So Mike and Ed were mates, and had set up a relatively different façade then in Huddersfield to regard for their lives together. And if they — seen at the musicale — were mates, utmost presumably Eileen and Mareeka — seen at Sinaia were mates too. And the rest? Was it Roland Kershaw and Terry, and Laura Perceval and Ursula? Gerald sat pondering.

He'd felt great sympathy for the couples. He and his woman had had no children, though they were only beginning to talk of relinquishment or fostering when his woman came ill. But relinquishment of the kind that Robbie was organizing presented issues of heart that he'd noway considered except in end, and he honored that now he was forced to scuffle with them in humorless. Was it in the child's interest — indeed granted the dreadful conditions in some of the orphanages to be espoused by a homosexual couple? What if, in some cases, they were pedophiles?

He was still muddled, thrashing around, when he got home. It sounded like an auspice to find a thick Ministry letter from Romania on his jellyfish, and further of an auspice still when he opened it the Ministry officers were impressed and pleased by the success of the stint, and wanted to have conversations aimed at publicizing them more extensively and making them more frequent. It was all Gerald demanded to make up his mind he checked his journal, also got on to Tarom at formerly to book a flight and a room at the Harmonia.

The aeroplane was late out of Heathrow as usual. When Gerald eventually made it to his hostel room he'd little energy left for a visit to the Panorama. The coming day was spent in addresses at the Ministry, addresses which alternated between the exhilarating and the frustrating as usual, but there was the difference this time that the atmosphere was specially more friendly. He ate beforehand at the Athenee Palace, hoping in vain to avoid the roadhouse, and also went back to the Harmonia.

" Is Mr. Taylor staying then at the moment? " he asked the new clerk at event, handsome and smiling.

" Robbie? Oh yes, he's then. He's always coming and going. It's room four- oh- eight. "

Upstairs the Panorama Bar was full of couples, and Radu ate him as a returned friend. Gerald set up a businessman he knew to talk to, and watched. All the couples or " couples, " as he allowed of them now were new, but they were going through the same routines which by now Gerald knew so well drinking beginners, encouraging the downhearted, comparing notes. And there too was Robbie, dashingly dressed as always, going from couple to couple, lines in hand, helping, directing, cheering. This wasn't the place, Gerald allowed, to talk to him.

It was after eleven, when all the couples had accepted his benediction and exhortation and drifted off, that Robbie left the bar. Gerald gave him ten twinkles, also went down to 408. The " Come in " was firm and confident.

" Oh, hello. I saw you were back. "

" I wonder if we could have a converse. "

" Sure. "

" You see, I went over to Huddersfield to see Mike and Mareeka. "

There was slightly a flicker of the eyelids. Robbie looked up at him unpretentiously, a small smile playing on his lips, hugely confident. holy, Gerald allowed suddenly.

" Oh yes. Mike telephoned and told me that someone had been there. Why do n't you sit down? "

Tentatively Gerald took the other president.

" So you see, I know all about this outfit of yours. "

" Do you? "

" Know that it's all a sham. How do you manage it? Forged passports? "

" Yes. "

“ Forged instruments of felicity for espousing? ”

“Occasionally. There are other ways with the private agencies, and occasionally with the Social Services people as well. ”

“All to put through dubious abdications for your own profit. I suppose Eileen and Mareeka are a couple, are they? ”

“ They are, as a matter of fact. Does it bother you? ”

“ No, it does n’t. But that’s not the point. And Roland and Terry. I suppose? And Laura and Ursula? ”

Robbie laughed out loud.

“ Sorry, old boy. You really do n’t know all about us after all. No, no Laura and Terry are a couple. ”

Gerald was baffled for a moment.

“ Oh? Why ca n’t they borrow in Britain? The age difference? ”

“ Not exactly. You see, they're family and family. ”

“ Oh... And Roland? ”

“ Roland is a bachelorette — a quiet man who’s lived alone all his life, and would now like to borrow a child. And Ursula is wedded — to a man with multiple sclerosis. They're comfortably out, and Ursula does n’t see why she should antedate the pleasure of having a child. So you see, it’s not as simple as you allowed. ”

“ No. ”

And yet Gerald wasn't sure that this new information made him feel less uneasy. Not with Robbie sitting there, that smile of tone- blessing playing on his lips. He was playing God reversing nature, righting wrongs, changing woe to bliss. And doing so to immense applause — from the people he backed, but also from himself. What kind of effect did playing God have on a man’s character? Gerald brought the matter bluntly into the open.

“ What gives you the right to play God? ”

“ You get me wrong. I do n’t play God. ” But he brushed away the blameworthiness with a despisement that was Olympian. “ I'm simply the facilitator. I make effects possible. ”

“ So what makes you suppose you know better than the trained social worker? ”

“ I know more because I do n’t have their narrow view of mortal eventuality. ”

“ How awful that sounds! But you do it for plutocrat. ”

“Incompletely. Romchild does make a modest profit. But substantially I do it to make people happy. There’s too little happiness around. ”

“ And if you set up that one of your... guests was a pedophile? Or a atrociousness? ”

“ I ’d call the whole thing off. I do have a bobby friend who's veritably good about checking if I've that dubitation... ” He leaned forward and raised his voice, like a politician. “ But when you suppose how numerous heads of children’s homes and foster parents have been set up to have abused the children in their care in recent times, do you suppose your notorious ‘ trained social workers ’ do so veritably much better than me? ”

It was a telling point. Gerald conceded it by standing up, irresolute, uneasy.

“ I do n’t know... I ’ll have to suppose. ”

“ And what might you do? ”

“ Go to the British police. You ’ve done several effects that are against British law. ”

Robbie shook his head.

“ I do n’t really suppose you ’re the kind of person who’s so conservative and prejudiced that you ’d want to stop me taking these children from the dreadful conditions they ’re living in. Have you seen any of them? They ’re vegetables where they are. And in Britain, in the homes I find for them, they ’re happy, laughing, normal children. I ’ve seen it. Women of forty-odd have children every day the world over. Why should n’t they borrow? Men bring up children on their own all the time when their women die or run out on them. Why should n’t they borrow? Yes, and homosexual couples too why should they be denied that joy? ”

It all made so important sense. It was just that Gerald, leaning against the hostel room door, doubted that air of premonition, that measureless tone- favor, that God- suchlike confidence.

And as he leaned his head against the door another picture came into Gerald’s mind of Robbie at the event office, his head and the event clerk’s bent over, studying passports, serious, upset. And he flashed back all that talk — orchestrated? a kind of medication? — about a rising drift of crime. And he flashed back that genial, sad, ordinary man, knifed in the dark thoroughfares as he went home from work.

“ You ’re relatively right, ” he said, keeping his voice as steady as possible. “ You ’re doing work that needs doing. You wo n’t hear any further from me. ”

Once clear of the room, in the dark stairwell that had given him such an creepy sensation of being watched indeed on his first day, he stopped and put his forepart against the gravestone wall. He'd still no idea what he was going to do. He didn't know whether he'd been believed or not. And if he hadn't been, he didn't know how far Robbie would go to keep him quiet. He'd entered one of those outlands which formerly he'd set up so intriguing, so instigative. And he did so veritably important want he had n’t.

www.ingramcontent.com/pod-product-compliance
Lightning Source LLC
LaVergne TN
LVHW080553160826
845677LV00010B/1832
* 9 7 9 8 3 5 6 9 3 1 8 5 7 *